ISBN: [9798343070576]

First Edition



The content of this book is for informational purposes only. The author has made every effort to ensure the accuracy of the information herein, but the content is provided "as is." The author and publisher assume no responsibility for errors or omissions or for any damages resulting from the use of the information contained in this book. The reader is encouraged to seek professional advice where appropriate.

# Table of Contents:

# Introduction: The Power of Decluttering

In a world that moves faster every day, where the pressures of work, relationships, and daily responsibilities seem to constantly mount, it's easy to find ourselves overwhelmed by the sheer volume of "stuff" in our lives. Not just physical items, but the mental, emotional, and digital clutter that accumulates over time. This clutter—both seen and unseen—can weigh us down, creating a sense of chaos that permeates every aspect of our existence. It's no wonder that so many of us feel stressed, anxious, and out of control. The good news is that there is a way to regain that control, to restore order and calm to our lives, and to pave the way for a more fulfilling and successful future. The answer lies in decluttering.

# What Is Decluttering, really?

When we think of decluttering, we often picture cleaning out our closets, organizing our kitchens, or tidying up our living spaces. While these are certainly important aspects of the process, decluttering is much more than just tidying up. It is about creating a life that is intentional and focused, where everything in your environment serves a purpose and contributes to your overall well-being.

Decluttering is not just about getting rid of things; it's about making space—space for the things that truly matter. It's about stripping away the excess so that you can focus on what brings you joy, enhances your health, improves your relationships, and amplifies your success. It's a holistic approach that encompasses your physical space, your mental landscape, your emotional well-being, and even your financial health.

## Why Decluttering Matters

The impact of clutter on our lives is profound. Clutter can create physical chaos, making it difficult to find things, complete tasks, or even relax in your own home. But it goes deeper than that. Clutter also affects our mental and emotional health. The constant visual reminder of unfinished tasks, the overwhelming feeling of too much stuff, and the stress of disorganization all contribute to a mental load that can be difficult to bear.

When we live in a cluttered environment, it's as if we are constantly being reminded of everything we haven't done. This can lead to a feeling of being trapped, unable to move forward because we are weighed down by the past. Studies have shown that cluttered spaces can lead to increased levels of cortisol, the stress hormone, which can have a range of negative effects on our health, from anxiety and depression to poor sleep and weight gain.

Moreover, clutter doesn't just affect us on an individual level. It also impacts our relationships. When our homes are cluttered, it can create tension between family members, leading to arguments and strained interactions. It can make us feel embarrassed to have people over, causing us to withdraw and isolate ourselves. In a cluttered environment, there's little room for relaxation, connection, and intimacy—the very things that strengthen our bonds with others.

And then there's the impact on our success. Whether we realize it or not, clutter can hold us back professionally. A cluttered workspace can lead to decreased productivity, making it harder to focus, meet deadlines, and achieve our goals. It can also create a sense of overwhelm that prevents us from taking on new opportunities or pursuing our dreams.

## The Benefits of a Decluttered Life

Now, imagine the opposite. Picture a home where everything has its place, where you can easily find what you need, and where your surroundings bring you peace rather than stress. Imagine a mind that is clear and focused, able to think creatively and solve problems with ease. Imagine relationships that are strong and fulfilling, free from the strain that clutter can cause. Imagine a life where you are able to pursue your goals with clarity and determination, unencumbered by the distractions of a cluttered environment.

This is the power of decluttering. By clearing away the excess, you create space for the things that truly matter. You create an environment that supports your well-being rather than detracting from it. You make room for growth, both personally and professionally.

Decluttering allows you to:

1. **Enhance Your Relationships**: A clutter-free environment fosters better communication, reduces stress, and creates space for connection and intimacy. It allows you to focus on the people in your life, rather than the stuff that surrounds you.

2. **Improve Your Health**: When your environment is organized and clutter-free, you are less likely to experience the stress and anxiety that clutter can cause. This can lead to better sleep, improved

mental health, and even better physical health as you are more likely to make healthy choices when your surroundings are in order.

3. **Amplify Your Success**: A decluttered workspace can lead to increased productivity, creativity, and focus. It can also boost your confidence and motivation, making it easier to achieve your goals and pursue new opportunities.

4. **Find Peace of Mind**: Decluttering isn't just about your physical space; it's also about decluttering your mind. When you clear away the mental clutter, you create space for clarity, focus, and peace. You are better able to make decisions, solve problems, and enjoy life.

# What You Will Learn in This Book

"Declutter Your Life: Say Goodbye to Chaos—How Decluttering Can Enhance Your Relationships, Improve Your Health, and Amplify Your Success" is your comprehensive guide to transforming your life through the power of decluttering. In the chapters that follow, we will take a deep dive into each aspect of decluttering, from your home to your mind, your relationships, your health, and even your finances.

- **Chapter 1** will start by helping you understand clutter in all its forms—physical, mental, emotional, and digital—and how it impacts your life.

- **Chapter 2** will guide you through the mindset shifts necessary to begin your decluttering journey, helping you overcome the barriers that have kept you stuck in clutter.

- **Chapter 3** will focus on decluttering your home, providing you with a room-by-room guide to creating a space that is organized, functional, and peaceful.

- **Chapter 4** will tackle the issue of mental clutter, offering strategies for clearing your mind and improving your focus and well-being.

- **Chapter 5** will explore the impact of clutter on your relationships and offer practical steps for decluttering your interactions and connections with others.

- **Chapter 6** will delve into the relationship between clutter and health, showing you how a clutter-free environment can lead to better physical and mental health.

- **Chapter 7** will address financial clutter, helping you to organize your finances, reduce stress, and achieve greater financial freedom.

- **Chapter 8** will show you how decluttering can amplify your success, with strategies for increasing productivity, achieving your goals, and living a more fulfilling life.

# Why Now Is the Time to Declutter

There's no better time than now to start your decluttering journey. As our lives become increasingly busy and complex, the need for simplicity and order becomes more apparent. By taking the time to declutter, you are making a commitment to yourself and to your future. You are choosing to prioritize your well-being, your relationships, and your success.

The process may seem daunting at first, but remember that you don't have to do it all at once. Decluttering is a journey, not a destination. Take it one step at a time, and celebrate your progress along the way. With each item you let go of, with each space you clear, you are creating a life that is more intentional, more focused, and more aligned with your true desires.

So, are you ready to say goodbye to chaos? Are you ready to embrace the power of decluttering and transform your life? If so, let's get started.

# Chapter 1: Understanding Clutter—More Than Just Stuff

# Section 1: Defining Clutter—It's Not Just Physical

When most people think of clutter, they envision piles of papers, overflowing closets, and garages so full that the car hasn't seen the inside in years. While these are certainly forms of clutter, they represent just one piece of the larger puzzle. Clutter can manifest in various aspects of our lives—mental, emotional, and digital—that are just as detrimental, if not more so, than physical clutter. To truly declutter your life, it's essential to recognize and address all forms of clutter.

## Physical Clutter: More Than Just a Mess

Physical clutter is the most visible form of clutter, and it's often where people start when they begin the process of decluttering. It's the stuff you can see and touch—the items that crowd your countertops, fill your drawers, and spill out of your closets. But physical clutter isn't just about messiness; it's about the impact these items have on your daily life.

Take Jane, for example. Jane was a busy mother of three who worked full-time and always felt like she was running on empty. Her home was filled with stuff—clothes the kids had outgrown, kitchen gadgets she never used, and stacks of unread magazines. Every time she walked into her living room, she felt overwhelmed by the sheer amount of things surrounding her. Even when she had time to relax, she couldn't fully unwind because the clutter was a constant reminder of everything she needed to do.

Jane's story is not unique. Many people experience a similar sense of overwhelm when faced with physical clutter. It's not just the mess that's the problem; it's what the mess represents—a lack of control, unfinished tasks, and a constant reminder of what's not being done. This can lead to chronic stress and a feeling of being trapped in your own home.

**Practical Advice for Tackling Physical Clutter:**

1. **Start Small:** The prospect of decluttering your entire home can be overwhelming. Instead, start with a small area, like a single drawer or a corner of a room. This allows you to build momentum and see immediate results, which can motivate you to continue.

2. **The Four-Box Method:** As you declutter, use four boxes labelled "Keep," "Donate," "Trash," and "Relocate." This method forces you to make decisions about each item rather than moving things from one place to another without actually reducing clutter.

3. **One In, One Out:** To prevent clutter from accumulating again, adopt the "one in, one out" rule. Every time you bring a new item into your home, commit to removing an old one. This helps maintain balance and prevents the buildup of unnecessary items.

4. **Declutter Regularly:** Decluttering isn't a one-time event. Make it a regular part of your routine—whether it's a weekly, monthly, or seasonal task—to keep physical clutter at bay.

By systematically addressing physical clutter, you create a living space that's not just tidy but also functional and peaceful. The goal is to have a home where everything has a place and everything you own serves a purpose, contributing to your overall well-being.

## Mental Clutter: The Invisible Burden

While physical clutter is easy to spot, mental clutter is more insidious. It's the thoughts, worries, and distractions that crowd your mind, making it difficult to focus or relax. Mental clutter often goes unnoticed until it starts to affect your productivity, decision-making, and overall mental health.

Consider Mark, a successful entrepreneur who was always busy. Mark's mind was constantly racing with thoughts of upcoming meetings, deadlines, and the next big idea for his business. Even when he tried to relax at home, he couldn't shut off his brain. His to-do list was never-ending, and the mental clutter kept him up at night, robbing him of the rest he desperately needed.

Mark's story highlights a common issue in today's fast-paced world. We live in a society that values busyness, and as a result, our minds are constantly bombarded with information, tasks, and decisions. This mental clutter can lead to burnout, anxiety, and a diminished ability to think clearly and creatively.

## Practical Advice for Clearing Mental Clutter:

1. **Mind Dumping:** One effective way to clear mental clutter is through mind dumping. Set aside a few minutes each day to write down everything that's on your mind—tasks, worries, ideas, and anything else taking up mental space. This process helps you get thoughts out of your head and onto paper, where you can prioritize and address them more effectively.

2. **Prioritization:** Not all tasks and thoughts are created equal. Learn to prioritize by identifying what's truly important and what can wait or be eliminated. Tools like the Eisenhower Matrix, which divides tasks into urgent, important, not urgent, and not important categories, can help you focus on what matters most.

3. **Mindfulness and Meditation:** Practicing mindfulness or meditation can help you declutter your mind by training you to focus on the present moment. Even a few minutes of mindfulness each day can reduce stress and improve mental clarity.

4. **Set Boundaries:** Mental clutter often accumulates because we don't set clear boundaries around our time and attention. Learn to say no to non-essential tasks and distractions, and create dedicated time for focus and relaxation.

Clearing mental clutter is about creating mental space to think, plan, and relax without being constantly overwhelmed by thoughts and worries. By decluttering your mind, you can improve your focus, reduce stress, and enhance your overall mental well-being.

## Emotional Clutter: The Weight of Unresolved Feelings

Emotional clutter is the baggage we carry from past experiences, unresolved conflicts, and unprocessed emotions. It's the anger, guilt, sadness, or anxiety that lingers in the background of our lives, affecting how we interact with others and how we see ourselves.

Sarah's story illustrates the impact of emotional clutter. After a painful breakup, Sarah struggled to move on. She kept mementos from the relationship—photos, gifts, and letters—all stored away in a box she rarely opened but couldn't bring herself to discard. These items represented unresolved emotions that she hadn't fully processed. Every time she saw the box, she was reminded of the past, making it difficult for her to fully embrace the present and open herself up to new relationships.

Emotional clutter, like Sarah's, can prevent us from moving forward in life. It keeps us tied to the past, often in ways that are harmful or limiting. This clutter can manifest in various forms, from holding onto physical items that carry emotional weight to avoiding difficult conversations that need to happen.

**Practical Advice for Addressing Emotional Clutter:**

1. **Identify Emotional Triggers:** Take time to identify the things in your life that trigger negative emotions. This could be certain items, people, or situations. Understanding what triggers these emotions is the first step toward addressing them.

2. **Letting Go Rituals:** If you're holding onto physical items that carry emotional weight, consider a letting-go ritual. This could involve writing a letter to yourself or the person associated with the item, expressing your feelings, and then physically letting

go of the item—either by donating, selling, or discarding it.

3. **Seek Closure:** Unresolved emotions often linger because we haven't sought closure. This might involve having a difficult conversation, seeking forgiveness, or simply accepting that some things are beyond our control. Therapy or counselling can be incredibly helpful in processing and letting go of emotional clutter.

4. **Practice Self-Compassion:** Emotional clutter often involves feelings of guilt, shame, or regret. Practicing self-compassion—treating yourself with kindness and understanding rather than harsh judgment—can help you release these negative emotions and move forward.

By addressing emotional clutter, you free yourself from the weight of the past and create space for healthier, more fulfilling relationships and a greater sense of emotional well-being.

## Digital Clutter: The Hidden Time Thief

In today's digital age, clutter isn't confined to our physical spaces or our minds. It has also invaded our digital lives. Digital clutter includes everything from an overflowing email inbox and disorganized files to the countless apps on your phone and the endless stream of notifications that demand your attention.

Let's look at Tom, a graphic designer who worked from home. Tom's computer desktop was a mess of files, his email inbox was constantly full, and his phone buzzed with notifications from various apps throughout the day. Despite being highly skilled at his job, Tom found it increasingly difficult to stay organized and focused. The digital clutter was a constant distraction, eating away at his productivity and peace of mind.

Tom's experience is a common one. Digital clutter may not take up physical space, but it can be just as disruptive. It can lead to wasted time as you search for files or sort through emails, and it can create a sense of overwhelm as you try to keep up with the constant barrage of information.

## Practical Advice for Reducing Digital Clutter:

1. **Inbox Zero:** Aim to achieve "inbox zero" by regularly clearing out your email inbox. Unsubscribe from newsletters and promotional emails you no longer read, and create folders or labels to organize important emails. Set aside specific times during the day to check and respond to emails, rather than allowing them to interrupt you constantly.

2. **File Organization:** Develop a consistent system for organizing your digital files. Create folders that are clearly labelled and easy to navigate. Regularly declutter your digital files by deleting or archiving those you no longer need. Backup important files to avoid losing them.

3. **App Audit:** Periodically review the apps on your phone and computer. Delete any that you no longer use or that don't add value to your life. Consider turning off notifications for non-essential apps to reduce distractions.

4. **Digital Detox:** Implement regular digital detoxes, where you disconnect from your devices for a set

period of time. This could be a few hours each day, a full day each week, or a weekend once a month. A digital detox can help you reset, reduce stress, and reconnect with the non-digital aspects of your life.

Reducing digital clutter is about reclaiming your time and attention. By creating a more organized and intentional digital environment, you can improve your productivity, reduce stress, and spend more time on activities that truly matter.

# Section 2: The Psychology of Clutter— Why We Hold On

Clutter isn't just about the accumulation of stuff; it's deeply tied to our emotions, fears, and sense of self. Understanding the psychological reasons behind why we hold on to clutter is crucial for addressing it effectively. This section delves into the emotional and mental barriers that prevent us from letting go of clutter, focusing on sentimental attachment, fear of loss, procrastination and avoidance, and the role of identity and status. By exploring these psychological factors, we can develop practical strategies to overcome them.

## Sentimental Attachment: When Memories Become Tangible

Sentimental attachment is one of the most powerful reasons people hold on to clutter. Objects become imbued with memories, emotions, and significance, making it difficult to let go. This attachment often goes beyond mere nostalgia; it's about preserving a connection to the past and the people or experiences associated with it.

Consider Emily's story. Emily inherited her grandmother's house, which was filled with items that held sentimental value—a set of old teacups, a worn-out armchair, and boxes of letters and photographs. Each item reminded her of her grandmother and the times they spent together. However, as much as Emily loved her grandmother, the sheer volume of items overwhelmed her. The house was cluttered to the point where it was difficult to move around, and yet, she couldn't bring herself to part with anything. Each item felt like a piece of her grandmother, and letting go felt like losing her all over again.

Emily's dilemma is a common one. Sentimental attachment often makes us hold on to items far longer than necessary, even when they no longer serve a practical purpose. The key is to find a balance between honouring memories and maintaining a functional, clutter-free environment.

**Practical Advice for Managing Sentimental Attachment:**

1. **Choose Representative Items:** Instead of keeping every item that holds sentimental value, choose a few representative items that encapsulate the memories. For example, instead of keeping all your grandmother's belongings, you might keep

just one or two items that are most meaningful to you, like a favourite photo or a cherished piece of jewellery.

2.  **Create a Memory Box:** Designate a specific box or space for sentimental items. This way, you can keep a limited number of items that hold emotional significance without allowing them to take over your entire living space. When the box is full, it's time to reassess and decide what's truly important.

3.  **Digitize Memories:** For items like photos, letters, or artwork, consider digitizing them. This allows you to preserve the memory without the physical clutter. You can scan photos and documents, and even create digital albums that you can revisit whenever you want, without taking up physical space.

4.  **Honor the Memory in Other Ways:** Sometimes, holding on to an item isn't the only way to honour a memory. Consider creating a scrapbook, writing a journal entry, or making a donation in honour of the person or event associated with the item. These actions can help you process the emotions and let go of the physical object.

By approaching sentimental items with intention and thoughtfulness, you can maintain a connection to your memories without allowing them to clutter your life. It's about finding ways to honour the past while making room for the present.

## Fear of Loss: The What-Ifs That Hold Us Back

The fear of loss is another powerful psychological barrier to decluttering. This fear often manifests as the "what-if" mindset—what if I need this someday? What if I can't find something like this again? What if I regret getting rid of it? These fears can cause us to hold on to items that no longer serve a purpose, out of a sense of security or safety.

Take Ben, for example. Ben had an entire garage filled with tools, old furniture, and boxes of miscellaneous items. Many of these things hadn't been used in years, but Ben couldn't bring himself to get rid of them. He was constantly thinking, "What if I need this tool for a project in the future?" or "What if this piece of furniture could be refurbished one day?" The fear of letting go, and the potential future need, kept his garage—and, by extension, his life—cluttered.

This fear of loss is rooted in the uncertainty of the future. We hold on to things because they provide a sense of comfort and preparedness. However, this mindset can also trap us in a cycle of accumulation, where the potential future use of an item outweighs its actual current value in our lives.

**Practical Advice for Overcoming the Fear of Loss:**

1. **Set a Usage Deadline:** For items you're holding on to "just in case," set a specific deadline for their use. If you haven't used the item within that time frame (e.g., six months or a year), it's a sign that it's not essential and can be let go.

2. **Assess the True Value:** Ask yourself whether the item is truly irreplaceable. In many cases, items we hold on to out of fear can easily be replaced if needed. Consider the cost and effort of replacing the item versus the space and peace of mind gained by letting it go.

3. **Create a "What-If" Box:** For items you're struggling to part with due to the fear of future need, place them in a "what-if" box. Seal the box and store it out of sight for a set period of time. If

you don't need to access the box during that period, it's likely safe to let go of the items inside.

4. **Embrace Minimalism:** Minimalism is about living with less and finding freedom in letting go. Embracing a minimalist mindset can help shift your focus from "what if" to "what's essential." By prioritizing quality over quantity, you can reduce the fear of loss and make more intentional decisions about what to keep.

By addressing the fear of loss head-on, you can begin to let go of items that are no longer serving you, creating space for what truly matters in your life. It's about trusting that you have enough and that you can handle whatever the future brings without holding on to unnecessary clutter.

## Procrastination and Avoidance: The Perfectionism Trap

Procrastination and avoidance are common reasons why clutter accumulates. Decluttering can be a daunting task, and the sheer scale of it can lead to feelings of overwhelm. This often results in procrastination—putting off the task because it seems too difficult or time-consuming. For some, the root of this procrastination is perfectionism—the fear that if the decluttering process isn't done perfectly, it's not worth doing at all.

Laura's story is a prime example of how procrastination and perfectionism can contribute to clutter. Laura had always been a perfectionist, and the idea of decluttering her home was overwhelming. She wanted to organize everything perfectly, but the thought of not being able to do it "right" made her put off the task for years. As a result, clutter continued to build up, creating a cycle of avoidance that became harder to break with time.

Procrastination is often a defence mechanism to avoid the discomfort of making decisions about what to keep and what to discard. This avoidance can lead to clutter piling up, as the task becomes increasingly daunting the longer it's delayed.

## Practical Advice for Combating Procrastination and Avoidance:

1. **Break It Down:** One of the most effective ways to overcome procrastination is to break the task into smaller, manageable steps. Instead of tackling an entire room at once, start with a single drawer or shelf. Completing these smaller tasks can build momentum and make the larger task seem less intimidating.

2. **Set a Timer:** Use the "Pomodoro Technique" by setting a timer for 25 minutes and focusing on decluttering during that time. After the timer goes off, take a five-minute break. This method helps you stay focused and reduces the tendency to procrastinate by creating a sense of urgency.

3. **Embrace Imperfection:** Recognize that decluttering doesn't have to be perfect. The goal is progress, not perfection. It's okay to make mistakes or to not have everything organized perfectly. What matters is that you're taking steps toward reducing clutter and improving your living space.

4. **Accountability:** Having someone to hold you accountable can be a powerful motivator. This could be a friend, family member, or professional organizer. By sharing your goals and progress with someone else, you create a sense of responsibility that can help you stay on track.

Overcoming procrastination and avoidance is about taking action, even if it's imperfect. By breaking the task into smaller steps and focusing on progress rather than perfection, you can start to make meaningful changes in your environment and reduce the clutter that's been holding you back.

## Identity and Status: The Things That Define Us

Clutter isn't just about the stuff we accumulate; it's also about what that stuff represents. For many people, clutter is tied to their identity and status. The items we own can become symbols of who we are—or who we aspire to be—and letting go of them can feel like losing a part of ourselves.

Take Chris, for example. Chris was a successful lawyer who prided himself on his professional achievements. His home office was filled with books, awards, and gadgets that symbolized his status and success. Over time, however, these items began to pile up, creating a cluttered and chaotic space. Despite the mess, Chris couldn't bring himself to part with anything. These items weren't just things; they were a reflection of his identity and accomplishments.

This connection between identity and possessions is deeply ingrained in our culture. We often equate our worth with what we own, leading to the accumulation of items that we believe signify success, status, or personal identity. However, this mindset can trap us in a cycle of consumption and clutter, where our possessions start to own us rather than the other way around.

**Practical Advice for Reframing Identity and Status:**

1. **Shift Your Perspective:** Start by shifting your perspective on what defines you. Your worth isn't determined by what you own, but by who you are and the values you live by. Focus on experiences, relationships, and personal growth rather than material possessions as markers of your identity and success.

2. **Quality Over Quantity:** Embrace the idea of quality over quantity. Instead of accumulating items that you believe signify status, invest in a few high-quality pieces that truly reflect your values and style. This can help reduce clutter and create a more intentional, meaningful environment.

3. **Detach from Labels:** Let go of the need to label yourself based on what you own. Instead of identifying as someone who has the latest gadgets or the biggest collection, focus on the qualities that truly define you—kindness, creativity, intelligence, or resilience.

4. **Redefine Success:** Redefine what success means to you. Instead of measuring success by the number of possessions or achievements, consider success in terms of personal fulfilment, happiness, and contribution to others. This shift can help you let go of items that no longer serve you and create a more clutter-free life.

# Section 3: The Impact of Clutter—How It Affects Your Life

Clutter isn't just an eyesore; it can have profound effects on various aspects of your life, often in ways that aren't immediately obvious. Whether it's the strain on your mental health, the toll on your relationships, the drag on your productivity, or even the impact on your physical health and finances, clutter can seep into every corner of your life. Understanding these impacts is the first step toward making meaningful changes. This section will explore how clutter affects mental health, relationships, productivity, physical health, and financial well-being, providing practical advice along the way.

## Mental Health: The Hidden Weight of Clutter

Clutter can have a significant impact on mental health, contributing to feelings of stress, anxiety, and depression. The connection between clutter and mental well-being is supported by research, which shows that a cluttered environment can lead to heightened levels of cortisol, the stress hormone. Living in a disorganized space can create a sense of chaos and overwhelm, making it difficult to relax and unwind.

Consider the story of Sarah, a mother of two who struggled with anxiety. Her home was filled with piles of laundry, stacks of papers, and an overflowing kitchen counter. Every time she walked through her house, she felt a growing sense of unease. The clutter was a constant reminder of all the unfinished tasks and responsibilities she had yet to tackle. This constant visual reminder of chaos made it difficult for Sarah to find peace of mind, contributing to her anxiety.

The mental load of clutter goes beyond just feeling stressed or anxious. It can also affect your cognitive function. Studies have shown that clutter can reduce your ability to focus and process information, leading to decreased productivity and decision-making abilities. When your environment is cluttered, your mind is likely to follow suit, making it harder to concentrate on tasks or think clearly.

**Practical Advice for Addressing Mental Health and Clutter:**

1. **Start Small:** If the idea of decluttering your entire home feels overwhelming, start with just one area—perhaps your bedroom or a small corner of your living room. Creating a clutter-free space

where you can relax and unwind can have a significant positive impact on your mental health.

2. **Establish Daily Habits:** Incorporate small decluttering tasks into your daily routine. This could be as simple as spending 10 minutes each morning tidying up your living room or organizing your desk at the end of the day. These small habits can prevent clutter from building up and help maintain a sense of order.

3. **Create a Calming Space:** Designate a clutter-free zone in your home where you can go to relax and decompress. This space should be free from distractions and clutter, allowing you to focus on self-care activities like reading, meditating, or practicing mindfulness.

4. **Seek Support:** If clutter is contributing to significant stress or anxiety, don't hesitate to seek support. This could be in the form of a professional organizer, a therapist, or a support group. Sometimes, having an outside perspective can help you see the situation more clearly and take actionable steps toward improvement.

By addressing the mental health impact of clutter, you can create a more peaceful and calming environment that supports your overall well-being. A clear space can lead to a clearer mind, reducing stress and improving your ability to focus and think clearly.

## Relationships: Clutter as a Barrier to Connection

Clutter doesn't just affect you; it can also strain your relationships with others. A cluttered home can create tension between family members, lead to embarrassment when inviting friends over, and even hinder your ability to form new relationships. When your space is filled with clutter, it can be difficult to connect with others on a meaningful level.

Imagine the story of John and Lisa, a couple who constantly argued about the state of their home. Lisa was a neat freak who couldn't stand the sight of clutter, while John was more laid-back and tended to accumulate things. Their differing attitudes toward clutter led to frequent arguments, with Lisa feeling overwhelmed and frustrated, and John feeling criticized and misunderstood. The clutter became a barrier between them, preventing them from enjoying their time together and causing a rift in their relationship.

Clutter can also lead to social isolation. When your home is cluttered, you might feel embarrassed to invite friends or family over, leading to a decrease in social interactions. This can contribute to feelings of loneliness and isolation, further exacerbating the negative impact of clutter on your well-being.

**Practical Advice for Improving Relationships and Reducing Clutter:**

1. **Communicate Openly:** If clutter is causing tension in your relationships, have an open and honest conversation about it. Discuss how the clutter makes you feel and work together to find solutions that work for everyone. It's important to approach the conversation with empathy and understanding, rather than blame or criticism.

2. **Set Boundaries:** Establish clear boundaries when it comes to clutter in shared spaces. For example, you might agree to keep the living room and kitchen clutter-free, while allowing for more flexibility in personal spaces like bedrooms or home offices. This can help reduce conflict and create a more harmonious living environment.

3. **Involve Everyone:** Make decluttering a family activity by involving everyone in the process. This can help build a sense of teamwork and shared responsibility, rather than placing the burden on one person. You can also turn it into a fun activity by setting goals or rewards for decluttering certain areas of the home.

4. **Create a Welcoming Environment:** Focus on creating a clutter-free space that feels welcoming and inviting to others. This could mean organizing your entryway, decluttering your living room, or setting up a cozy seating area. A clean and organized space can make it easier to connect with others and enjoy social interactions.

By reducing clutter and addressing its impact on your relationships, you can create a more positive and supportive environment at home. This can lead to stronger connections with loved ones and a greater sense of belonging.

**Productivity: Clutter as a Distraction**

Clutter is a significant barrier to productivity, both at home and in the workplace. A cluttered environment can make it difficult to focus, leading to decreased efficiency and a constant feeling of being "busy" without actually getting much done. The visual noise created by clutter can pull your attention in multiple directions, making it challenging to concentrate on a single task.

Consider the story of Mark, a freelance writer who worked from home. Mark's desk was covered in papers, books, and miscellaneous items, making it difficult for him to find what he needed when he needed it. As a result, he spent a significant amount of time searching for documents, getting distracted by other tasks, and feeling overwhelmed by the sheer volume of stuff on his desk. This cluttered environment led to procrastination and decreased productivity, making it harder for Mark to meet his deadlines and produce high-quality work.

The impact of clutter on productivity is well-documented. Research has shown that a cluttered workspace can reduce your ability to focus, process information, and complete tasks efficiently. Clutter can also lead to increased stress and anxiety, further hindering your ability to be productive.

**Practical Advice for Boosting Productivity by Reducing Clutter:**

1. **Create a Dedicated Workspace:** Designate a specific area in your home for work or productive activities. Keep this space free from distractions and clutter, allowing you to focus on the task at hand. A clean and organized workspace can help you feel more in control and boost your productivity.

2. **Implement a "One-Touch" Rule:** To prevent clutter from building up, implement a "one-touch" rule, where you handle items only once. For example, instead of setting a piece of paper aside to deal with later, take action on it immediately—file it, recycle it, or complete the task it represents. This can help reduce the accumulation of clutter and keep your workspace organized.

3. **Set Up Organizational Systems:** Invest in organizational tools and systems that can help you keep your workspace tidy. This could include filing cabinets, drawer organizers, or digital tools for managing documents and tasks. Having a system in

place can make it easier to maintain an organized and clutter-free workspace.

4. **Declutter Regularly:** Make it a habit to declutter your workspace regularly. This could be a weekly or monthly routine where you go through your desk, files, and other work-related items to clear out anything that's no longer needed. Regular decluttering can prevent clutter from building up and keep your workspace conducive to productivity.

By addressing the impact of clutter on productivity, you can create a more efficient and effective work environment. A clutter-free space can help you focus, reduce stress, and accomplish more in less time.

## Physical Health: The Hidden Hazards of Clutter

Clutter doesn't just affect your mental and emotional well-being; it can also have serious consequences for your physical health. A cluttered environment can create safety hazards, contribute to poor hygiene, and even exacerbate chronic health conditions like asthma and allergies.

Take the story of Janet, an older woman who lived alone in a cluttered house. Over the years, Janet had accumulated so many belongings that her home became difficult to navigate. Piles of magazines, boxes, and other items created tripping hazards, and her kitchen was so cluttered that it was challenging to prepare healthy meals. One day, Janet tripped over a box and fell, resulting in a broken hip. This incident was a wake-up call for Janet, who realized that her cluttered environment was putting her health and safety at risk.

In addition to safety hazards, clutter can also contribute to poor indoor air quality. Dust, mold, and allergens can accumulate in cluttered spaces, leading to respiratory issues and other health problems. Clutter can also make it difficult to clean and maintain a healthy living environment, increasing the risk of pests and other health hazards.

**Practical Advice for Protecting Physical Health by Reducing Clutter:**

1. **Prioritize Safety:** Take a close look at your home and identify any safety hazards created by clutter. This could include tripping hazards, blocked exits, or items that could fall and cause injury. Address

these hazards by decluttering and reorganizing your space to ensure it's safe and easy to navigate.

2. **Improve Air Quality:** Reduce the accumulation of dust and allergens by regularly cleaning and decluttering your home. Pay special attention to areas where clutter tends to build up, such as closets, basements, and attics. Consider using air purifiers or other tools to improve indoor air quality and protect your respiratory health.

3. **Create a Healthy Kitchen:** A cluttered kitchen can make it difficult to prepare healthy meals, leading to poor eating habits and health outcomes. Declutter your kitchen by clearing out old or unused items, organizing your pantry, and creating designated spaces for meal preparation. A clean and organized kitchen can make it easier to cook healthy meals and maintain a balanced diet.

4. **Seek Professional Help:** If clutter is creating significant health risks in your home, consider seeking professional help. A professional organizer or a cleaning service can assist you in decluttering and creating a safer living environment.

By reducing clutter and addressing its impact on your physical health, you can create a safer and healthier home environment. This can lead to improved well-being and a reduced risk of accidents and health issues.

## Financial Impact: The Cost of Clutter

Clutter can also have a significant financial impact, often in ways that aren't immediately obvious. The costs associated with clutter can add up over time, from the money spent on unnecessary items to the expenses incurred from storing or maintaining them.

Consider the story of Tom, who loved to shop and frequently bought new gadgets and clothes. Over time, his home became filled with items he didn't need or use. Tom also had a habit of misplacing things, leading him to buy replacements for items he already owned. This cycle of buying and accumulating led to financial strain, as Tom found himself struggling to keep up with credit card bills and other expenses.

Clutter can also lead to financial waste in other ways. For example, expired food hidden in the back of a cluttered pantry, late fees on bills that got lost in a pile of papers, or the cost of renting a storage unit to hold items that no longer fit in your home. All of these expenses can add up, draining your financial resources and creating additional stress.

**Practical Advice for Reducing the Financial Impact of Clutter:**

1. **Adopt a "One In, One Out" Rule:** To prevent clutter from accumulating, adopt a "one in, one out" rule, where you only bring new items into your home if you're willing to let go of something else. This can help you be more intentional about your purchases and reduce the financial impact of clutter.

2. **Sell or Donate Unused Items:** Instead of letting unused items take up space and accumulate dust, consider selling or donating them. This can help you recoup some of the money spent on those items and reduce the financial burden of clutter. Online marketplaces, garage sales, and donation centers are great options for getting rid of unwanted items.

3. **Avoid Impulse Purchases:** Be mindful of impulse purchases, which can quickly lead to clutter and

financial strain. Before making a purchase, ask yourself if you truly need the item and if it aligns with your values and goals. Taking a moment to reflect can help you avoid unnecessary spending and reduce clutter.

4.  **Create a Budget:** Establish a budget that includes a category for decluttering and home organization. This can help you allocate funds toward maintaining an organized space and prevent clutter-related financial waste. It can also serve as a reminder to be intentional about your spending and prioritize experiences and values over material possessions.

By addressing the financial impact of clutter, you can create a more intentional and sustainable approach to managing your belongings. This can lead to greater financial stability and a reduced burden of clutter-related expenses.

# Chapter 2: The Decluttering Mindset— Preparing for Transformation

# Section 1: Embracing the Power of Letting Go

Letting go is one of the most challenging aspects of decluttering. Our possessions often carry significant emotional weight, making it difficult to part with them even when we know they no longer serve us. However, learning to let go is crucial for creating a clutter-free life. In this section, we'll explore the reasons behind our emotional attachments to things, the benefits of letting go, and practical steps to help you embrace this essential part of the decluttering process.

**Understanding the Emotional Attachment to Stuff**

Our attachment to physical items is rooted in various emotional and psychological factors. These attachments can make it incredibly challenging to let go, even when we know it's in our best interest. Here are some of the most common reasons why we hold on to things:

1. **Sentimental Value:** Many items in our homes carry memories or represent important moments in our lives. A wedding dress, a child's first drawing, or a souvenir from a memorable trip can all hold

deep emotional significance. We fear that letting go of these items means letting go of the memories or the person they represent.

**Story Example:** Consider the case of Emma, a 40-year-old woman who had kept every greeting card she'd ever received. These cards, stored in multiple boxes in her attic, represented decades of friendships and family connections. Emma believed that discarding them would mean losing a piece of her past and dishonouring the relationships they symbolized.

2. **Fear of Scarcity:** Another common reason we hold on to items is the fear of scarcity—the idea that we might need something in the future and won't have it. This fear can lead to keeping items "just in case," even if they haven't been used in years.

**Story Example:** John, a retiree, had a garage full of old tools, outdated electronics, and spare parts. He rarely used these items but kept them because he feared that as soon as he got rid of something, he would need it the next day. This fear of needing something in the future kept John's garage cluttered and chaotic.

3. **Comfort and Security:** For some, clutter provides a sense of comfort and security. Possessions can act as a protective buffer against the uncertainties of life, creating a cocoon of familiarity. Letting go of items can feel like stepping into the unknown, which can be unsettling.

**Story Example:** Sarah, a busy mother of three, found herself holding onto baby clothes, toys, and other items long after her children had outgrown them. These items represented a time in her life that she cherished, and letting go felt like acknowledging that her children were growing up and that she was entering a new phase of life.

Understanding why you hold on to certain items is the first step in learning to let go. It's important to recognize that these attachments are natural but can also be limiting. Letting go doesn't mean erasing memories or abandoning security; it means making space for new experiences and possibilities.

## Shifting from Ownership to Freedom

The idea of letting go can be intimidating, but it's also incredibly liberating. When you release your grip on material possessions, you open up space—both physically and mentally—for new opportunities, experiences, and growth. Here's how shifting your mindset from ownership to freedom can transform your life:

1. **The Burden of Ownership:** Owning too many things can be a heavy burden. Every item in your home requires attention—whether it's cleaning, maintaining, or simply finding a place to store it. This burden can lead to feelings of overwhelm and exhaustion.

**Story Example:** Laura, a successful businesswoman, owned a large house filled with expensive furniture, art, and collectibles. While she loved these items, she often felt overwhelmed by the constant upkeep. Dusting the antiques, cleaning the numerous rooms, and organizing the collections became a chore that left her with little time to relax or pursue her passions.

2. **The Freedom of Simplicity:** Letting go of unnecessary possessions can create a sense of freedom and lightness. When you have fewer things, you have fewer responsibilities, which can lead to a more peaceful and fulfilling life.

**Story Example:** After years of feeling burdened by her possessions, Laura decided to downsize. She sold her large home and moved into a smaller, more manageable space. She kept only the items that truly brought her joy and found that the simpler lifestyle gave her more time to travel, spend with loved ones, and pursue hobbies she had previously neglected.

3. **Embracing Change:** Letting go of physical items can symbolize a willingness to embrace change and move forward. It's an acknowledgment that your identity and happiness aren't tied to material things but to the experiences, relationships, and personal growth that truly matter.

**Story Example:** When Sarah finally decided to donate her children's old toys and clothes, she felt a sense of relief. She realized that her memories of her children's early years weren't contained in those objects but in the experiences, they shared as a family. By letting go, she was able to fully embrace the next chapter of her life with gratitude and optimism.

Shifting your mindset from ownership to freedom is about recognizing that less can be more. When you let go of the things that no longer serve you, you make room for a life that's richer in meaning and purpose.

**Practical Steps to Start Letting Go**

Letting go is a process, and it's important to approach it with patience and compassion for yourself. Here are some practical steps to help you start embracing the power of letting go:

1. **Start with Low-Hanging Fruit:** Begin by decluttering areas of your home that don't carry significant emotional weight. This could be your bathroom, kitchen, or laundry room. Starting with these less emotionally charged spaces can build your confidence and momentum.

**Example:** If you're overwhelmed by the thought of decluttering your entire house, start with your bathroom cabinets. Throw away expired products, organize your toiletries, and create a space that's functional and clutter-free. This small win can motivate you to tackle more challenging areas.

2. **Use the "One-Year" Rule:** For items that you're unsure about, use the "one-year" rule—if you

haven't used or worn the item in the past year, it's likely that you won't use it in the future. This rule can help you make clearer decisions about what to keep and what to let go.

**Example:** John, who had a habit of keeping things "just in case," applied the one-year rule to his garage. He realized that many of the tools and spare parts hadn't been touched in years. By letting go of these items, he freed up space and reduced the clutter that had been causing him stress.

3. **Create a Memory Box:** For sentimental items that you're not ready to part with, consider creating a memory box. This allows you to keep a small, curated collection of meaningful items without letting them take over your living space.

**Example:** Emma, who had boxes of greeting cards, decided to create a memory box for the most meaningful ones. She kept a few cards from each important relationship and let go of the rest. This way, she honoured her memories without allowing them to clutter her home.

4. **Focus on the Benefits:** Remind yourself of the benefits of letting go—more space, less stress, greater freedom, and the ability to focus on what

truly matters. Keeping these benefits in mind can help you stay motivated throughout the process.

**Example:** Laura, who had downsized her home, kept a journal where she wrote about the positive changes she experienced after letting go of her excess possessions. She found that focusing on the benefits helped her stay committed to her simpler, clutter-free lifestyle.

5. **Set Boundaries:** Establish clear boundaries for what you bring into your home moving forward. This could mean adopting a "one in, one out" rule, where you only bring in a new item if you're willing to let go of something else. Setting these boundaries can prevent clutter from accumulating in the future.

**Example:** After decluttering her children's old toys, Sarah set a rule that for every new toy they received, they would donate an old one. This practice helped her maintain a clutter-free home and taught her children the value of generosity and simplicity.

6. **Seek Support:** If you're struggling to let go, don't hesitate to seek support from friends, family, or a professional organizer. Sometimes, having an outside perspective can help you see the situation

more clearly and give you the encouragement you
need to move forward.

**Example:** When Emma found it difficult to let go of
certain sentimental items, she enlisted the help of a close
friend who could provide an objective perspective. Her
friend helped her make decisions and offered emotional
support throughout the process.

# Section 2: Overcoming Mental Barriers to Decluttering

Decluttering is as much a mental exercise as it is a physical one. The mental barriers we create can often be the most challenging obstacles to overcome when trying to declutter our lives. Whether it's perfectionism, fear of making mistakes, procrastination, or deeply ingrained habits, these barriers can keep us stuck in a cycle of clutter and inaction. In this section, we'll explore common mental barriers to decluttering, provide practical advice on how to overcome them, and share real-life stories to make the concepts more relatable and engaging.

## Identifying Common Mental Blocks

Before we can overcome mental barriers, it's essential to identify them. Some of the most common mental blocks include:

1. **Perfectionism:** Perfectionism is the belief that everything must be done perfectly or not at all. This mindset can be paralyzing, making it difficult to start or complete decluttering tasks. Perfectionists

often fear that they won't do a good enough job, leading them to avoid the task altogether.

**Story Example:** Lisa, a graphic designer, struggled with perfectionism. Her home office was cluttered with design magazines, outdated equipment, and half-finished projects. Lisa kept telling herself that she needed to organize everything perfectly before she could start working, but the fear of not doing it right prevented her from even beginning.

2. **Fear of Making Mistakes:** Many people fear that they'll regret getting rid of something, leading them to hold onto items just in case they might need them someday. This fear of making mistakes can result in a cluttered home filled with items that are rarely, if ever, used.

**Story Example:** Tom, a retired teacher, had a basement full of old textbooks, lesson plans, and teaching aids. He feared that he might need these materials in the future, even though he had no plans to return to teaching. This fear of making a mistake kept him from letting go, even though the clutter was taking over his space.

3. **Procrastination:** Procrastination is a common barrier to decluttering. Many people put off decluttering tasks because they seem overwhelming or unpleasant. The longer they wait, the more daunting the task becomes, leading to a vicious cycle of avoidance.

**Story Example:** Maria, a busy nurse, knew that her closet was overflowing with clothes she no longer wore. However, she kept putting off the task of decluttering because it seemed like too much work. Each time she thought about it, she felt overwhelmed and decided to deal with it "later," which never seemed to come.

4. **Habits and Routine:** Our habits and routines can also be significant barriers to decluttering. We often become accustomed to our surroundings, even if they're cluttered, and changing these habits can be challenging. The comfort of routine can make it difficult to see the clutter for what it is—a barrier to a more organized and fulfilling life.

**Story Example:** Robert, a 60-year-old accountant, had a habit of collecting newspapers and magazines. Every morning, he would buy the paper and place it on a growing stack in his living room. This routine had become so ingrained that he didn't even notice how the pile of papers was taking over his space.

**Challenging Limiting Beliefs**

Once you've identified the mental barriers that are holding you back, the next step is to challenge and reframe the limiting beliefs that contribute to these barriers. Here's how to tackle each one:

1. **Overcoming Perfectionism: Progress Over Perfection**

**Reframe the Belief:** Instead of focusing on perfection, focus on progress. Remind yourself that decluttering doesn't have to be done perfectly to be effective. The goal is to create a space that works for you, not to achieve some unattainable ideal.

**Practical Advice:** Break tasks down into smaller, manageable steps. For example, instead of trying to declutter your entire office in one day, start with one drawer or one shelf. Celebrate each small victory, and remember that progress is more important than perfection.

**Story Example:** Lisa decided to start small by organizing one drawer in her office. She found that once she got started, it was easier to keep going. By focusing on progress rather than perfection, she was able to declutter her office over time, creating a space that was functional and inspiring.

## 2. Conquering the Fear of Making Mistakes: Trust Your Judgment

**Reframe the Belief:** Trust that you're capable of making good decisions about what to keep and what to let go. Remind yourself that most items can be replaced if absolutely necessary, but the mental and physical space you gain from decluttering is invaluable.

**Practical Advice:** Set clear criteria for what you will keep and what you will let go. For example, you might decide to keep only items that you've used in the past year or that have a clear purpose in your life. Trust your instincts and remember that letting go of items that no longer serve you is a positive step.

**Story Example:** Tom decided to trust his judgment and set a rule for his basement: if he hadn't used a teaching resource in the past five years, it was time to let it go. He donated most of his old teaching materials to a local school and felt a sense of relief and accomplishment. The fear of making a mistake had held him back for years, but trusting his judgment allowed him to reclaim his space.

### 3. Overcoming Procrastination: Start Small and Build Momentum

**Reframe the Belief:** Instead of viewing decluttering as an overwhelming task, see it as a series of small, manageable steps. Each step you take brings you closer to your goal, and once you start, momentum will carry you forward.

**Practical Advice:** Use the "Five-Minute Rule." Commit to spending just five minutes on a decluttering task. Once you start, you may find it easier to keep going. Even if you only declutter for five minutes, that's progress, and it's better than doing nothing.

**Story Example:** Maria decided to set a timer for five minutes and start with one section of her closet. Once she began, she found that it wasn't as difficult as she had imagined. She ended up spending 20 minutes sorting through her clothes and felt a sense of accomplishment afterward. By starting small, she was able to overcome her procrastination and make meaningful progress.

## 4. Breaking Habits and Routine: Create New Patterns

**Reframe the Belief:** Acknowledge that habits can be changed with intention and practice. Recognize that while routines provide comfort, they can also keep you stuck in unproductive patterns. Creating new, more beneficial habits can lead to a clutter-free environment.

**Practical Advice:** Start by changing one habit at a time. For example, if you have a habit of leaving papers on the table, create a new routine where you immediately file or discard them. It may take time to adjust, but with consistency, new habits will form.

**Story Example:** Robert realized that his habit of collecting newspapers was contributing to the clutter in his home. He decided to change his routine by reading the news online instead of buying physical papers. He also made a habit of recycling old newspapers weekly. Over time, his living room became more spacious, and he felt less overwhelmed by clutter.

## Building Resilience and Perseverance

Decluttering is not a one-time event; it's an ongoing process that requires resilience and perseverance. Here's how to stay motivated and maintain momentum throughout your decluttering journey:

1. **Set Realistic Goals:** Setting realistic goals is key to staying motivated. Break your decluttering projects into smaller tasks with specific, achievable goals. This approach makes the process less overwhelming and gives you a sense of accomplishment as you reach each milestone.

**Example:** Instead of setting a goal to declutter your entire home, break it down by room or even by category (e.g., clothing, books, kitchen items). Set a goal to declutter one room per month or one category per week. Achieving these smaller goals will keep you motivated and moving forward.

2. **Celebrate Small Wins:** Recognize and celebrate your progress, no matter how small. Every item you let go of and every space you declutter is a step in the right direction. Celebrating these small wins reinforces positive behaviour and keeps you motivated.

**Example:** After decluttering her closet, Maria treated herself to a new book she had been wanting to read. Celebrating this small win made her feel proud of her accomplishment and motivated her to continue decluttering other areas of her home.

3. **Stay Focused on the Bigger Picture:** Keep your end goal in mind—a clutter-free, organized, and peaceful living space. When the process feels challenging, remind yourself of the benefits you'll gain, such as reduced stress, increased productivity, and a more enjoyable home environment.

**Example:** Lisa kept a vision board in her office with images of beautifully organized workspaces. Whenever she felt overwhelmed or tempted to revert to her old habits, she would look at the board and remind herself of the clutter-free office she was working toward.

4. **Practice Self-Compassion:** Be kind to yourself throughout the decluttering process. Understand that it's normal to face challenges and setbacks. Practice self-compassion by acknowledging your efforts and progress, even if it's not perfect.

**Example:** When Tom felt frustrated that he couldn't let go of certain items in his basement, he reminded himself that decluttering is a journey, not a race. He allowed himself to take breaks when needed and returned to the task when he felt ready.

5. **Seek Accountability:** Having someone to support you can make a big difference in staying on track with your decluttering goals. Share your goals with a friend or family member, or join a decluttering group where you can exchange tips and encouragement.

**Example:** Robert joined an online decluttering group where members shared their progress and challenges. The accountability and support he received from the group helped him stay motivated and committed to his decluttering journey.

# Section 3: Cultivating a Vision for a Clutter-Free Life

Cultivating a vision for a clutter-free life is an essential step in your decluttering journey. A clear vision serves as a guiding light, helping you stay focused and motivated as you work toward creating a space that reflects your values and supports your well-being. In this section, we'll explore how to develop a meaningful vision, offer practical advice for turning that vision into reality, and share stories that demonstrate the transformative power of living clutter-free.

## Why a Vision Matters

A well-defined vision acts as a roadmap for your decluttering efforts. Without a vision, it's easy to lose direction, become overwhelmed, or fall back into old habits. Your vision should be more than just a vague desire for a tidy home; it should encapsulate how you want to feel in your space, the lifestyle you want to lead, and the values you want your environment to reflect.

**Story Example:** Sarah, a busy mother of three, felt constantly stressed and overwhelmed by the clutter in her home. Despite her best efforts to tidy up, the mess always seemed to return. It wasn't until she developed a clear vision of a peaceful, organized home—where her family could relax and enjoy quality time together—that she began to make lasting changes. Her vision kept her motivated during the decluttering process, reminding her of the calm and happiness she was working toward.

## Steps to Cultivating Your Vision

### 1. Reflect on Your Current Situation

Begin by assessing your current living environment. What areas of your home cause you the most stress? How does the clutter impact your daily life, relationships, and well-being? This reflection will help you identify the key areas that need attention and provide a starting point for your vision.

**Practical Advice:** Take a walk through your home with a notepad or your phone, and jot down your observations. Note how each room makes you feel and what changes you'd like to see. This exercise will help you become more aware of the impact of clutter and clarify your goals for a clutter-free space.

**Story Example:** When John, a freelance writer, took a walk through his cluttered apartment, he realized that the mess in his living room made it difficult to relax after a long day. His bedroom, which was supposed to be a sanctuary, felt more like a storage unit. These realizations motivated him to create a vision of a home that felt peaceful, inviting, and conducive to both work and rest.

## 2. Envision Your Ideal Space

Once you've identified the problem areas, it's time to envision your ideal space. Think about how you want your home to look, feel, and function. What kind of atmosphere do you want to create? What activities do you want to enjoy in each room? Your vision should be detailed and specific, reflecting your unique needs and desires.

**Practical Advice:** Create a vision board using images from magazines, Pinterest, or other sources that inspire you. Include pictures of organized spaces, color schemes you love, and anything that represents the lifestyle you want to cultivate. Keep this vision board somewhere you can see it daily as a reminder of what you're working toward.

**Story Example:** Emily, a schoolteacher, created a vision board for her home office. She included images of a clean desk, open shelves with neatly organized books, and a cozy reading nook. This vision helped her stay focused as she decluttered, guiding her decisions on what to keep and what to discard.

### 3.  **Connect Your Vision to Your Values**

Your vision for a clutter-free life should align with your core values. Whether it's spending more quality time with loved ones, prioritizing health and wellness, or pursuing a creative passion, your decluttering efforts should support these values. When your environment reflects what matters most to you, it becomes easier to maintain a clutter-free space.

**Practical Advice:** Take some time to reflect on your values and how they relate to your living environment. For example, if family is a top priority, your vision might include creating a clutter-free living room where everyone can gather comfortably. If health and wellness are important, you might focus on decluttering the kitchen to make healthy cooking more enjoyable.

**Story Example:** Laura, a fitness enthusiast, realized that her cluttered kitchen was hindering her ability to prepare healthy meals. She envisioned a kitchen with clear countertops, organized cabinets, and easy access to her cooking tools. By aligning her vision with her value of health, she was able to create a space that supported her wellness goals.

### 4.  Set Clear, Achievable Goals

With your vision in place, it's time to set clear, achievable goals that will help you bring that vision to life. These goals should be specific, measurable, and time-bound. For example, instead of setting a vague goal like "declutter the house," break it down into smaller, actionable steps, such as "organize the pantry by the end of the week."

**Practical Advice:** Use the SMART criteria (Specific, Measurable, Achievable, Relevant, Time-bound) to set your decluttering goals. For example, if your vision includes a serene bedroom, a SMART goal might be: "Sort through and donate unused clothing by Saturday, and rearrange the furniture to create a more relaxing layout by next weekend."

**Story Example:** David, an entrepreneur, wanted his home office to be a space of creativity and productivity. He set a SMART goal to declutter his desk by getting rid of old papers and organizing his supplies within two days.

Achieving this goal gave him the momentum to tackle other areas of his office, bringing him closer to his vision.

## Practical Strategies for Turning Your Vision into Reality

### 1.  Start with a Clean Slate

To fully embrace your vision, it's helpful to start with a clean slate. This might mean temporarily clearing out a room or space so that you can reimagine it without the distraction of clutter. Once you have a blank canvas, it's easier to see the potential and plan how to arrange and organize the space to match your vision.

**Practical Advice:** If possible, empty the room you're focusing on and give it a thorough cleaning. This fresh start can be incredibly motivating and will allow you to see the space in a new light. As you bring items back in, be selective, only keeping what fits with your vision.

**Story Example:** Lisa wanted to transform her cluttered living room into a calm, inviting space for her family to relax. She decided to remove all the furniture and decorations temporarily, giving the room a fresh start. As she brought items back in, she was intentional about keeping only what aligned with her vision, resulting in a beautifully organized space.

## 2. Adopt a "Less is More" Mentality

A key principle of a clutter-free life is the idea that less is more. This doesn't mean living with the bare minimum, but rather being intentional about what you choose to keep in your space. By embracing minimalism, you can create an environment that is both functional and aesthetically pleasing.

**Practical Advice:** As you declutter, ask yourself if each item truly adds value to your life. Does it serve a purpose or bring you joy? If not, consider letting it go. Remember, the goal is to create a space that supports your vision, not to hold onto things out of guilt or obligation.

**Story Example:** Mark, a photographer, had accumulated a large collection of camera equipment over the years. However, he realized that he only used a few pieces regularly. By adopting a "less is more" mentality, he sold the equipment he no longer used and invested in high-quality storage for the items he kept. This streamlined approach made his workspace more efficient and aligned with his vision of simplicity.

### 3.  Create Systems to Maintain Your Vision

Once you've achieved your clutter-free space, the next challenge is maintaining it. Creating systems and routines that support your vision is crucial for long-term success. These systems should be simple, sustainable, and tailored to your lifestyle.

**Practical Advice:** Establish daily and weekly routines to keep clutter at bay. For example, you might set aside 10 minutes each evening to tidy up or designate a specific day each week for deeper cleaning and organizing. Consistency is key to maintaining your vision over time.

**Story Example:** After decluttering her kitchen, Emily created a routine of cleaning up after each meal and setting aside Sunday afternoons for meal prep. These routines helped her maintain the organized space she had worked so hard to create, making it easier to stick to her healthy eating habits.

### 4.  Seek Inspiration and Support

Staying inspired and motivated is essential as you work toward your vision. Surround yourself with positive influences, whether it's through books, online communities, or friends who share your goals. Having support and accountability can make the process more enjoyable and rewarding.

**Practical Advice:** Join a decluttering or minimalism group online or in your community. Share your progress, challenges, and successes with others who are on a similar journey. The encouragement and ideas you gain from others can help keep you on track.

**Story Example:** Sarah joined a local decluttering group where members shared tips, resources, and success stories. The support she received from the group was invaluable, helping her stay motivated and committed to her vision of a peaceful, clutter-free home.

# Chapter 3: Decluttering Your Home—Creating a Sanctuary

# Section 1: Room-by-Room Decluttering Strategies

Decluttering your home room by room allows you to systematically transform each space into a functional, serene environment. Each room serves a different purpose, so it's essential to tailor your approach to the specific needs of the space. Here, we'll explore practical strategies for decluttering the kitchen, living room, bedroom, and bathroom, ensuring that each area becomes a true sanctuary.

## The Kitchen: Heart of the Home

The kitchen is often the busiest room in the house, where meals are prepared, and family and friends gather. However, it can quickly become cluttered with utensils, gadgets, and pantry items. A cluttered kitchen not only makes cooking more stressful but can also lead to food waste and frustration.

**Step 1: Clear the Countertops** Start by removing everything from the countertops. Only essential items, such as a coffee maker or a fruit bowl, should remain. Clearing your counters instantly makes the kitchen feel more spacious and less chaotic.

**Practical Tip:** Store frequently used items in easily accessible drawers or cabinets. Use organizers to keep utensils, spices, and cooking tools in order. For example, a lazy Susan in a corner cabinet can help you access spices without cluttering the countertop.

**Story Example:** Lisa, a busy mom, used to have every kitchen gadget she owned on her countertops. This clutter made meal prep overwhelming. After clearing her counters and storing gadgets in designated cabinets, she found cooking to be more enjoyable and efficient.

**Step 2: Declutter the Pantry and Cabinets** Pantries and cabinets are often filled with expired foods, duplicate items, and things we never use. Start by taking everything out and sorting items into categories: keep, donate, or discard.

**Practical Tip:** Use clear containers for dry goods to keep things organized and easy to see. Label each container, so you know exactly what you have. Arrange items by category and frequency of use—keep daily essentials at eye level and lesser-used items higher up.

**Story Example:** Sarah discovered expired spices and forgotten ingredients buried in the back of her pantry. By decluttering and organizing her pantry with clear containers and labels, she reduced food waste and made meal planning simpler.

**Step 3: Organize the Fridge and Freezer** A cluttered fridge makes it hard to find ingredients and leads to food spoilage. Take everything out, clean the shelves, and discard expired or unused items.

**Practical Tip:** Group similar items together—dairy on one shelf, condiments on another. Use bins to corral small items like yogurt or cheese. This organization makes it easier to see what you have and avoid overbuying.

**Story Example:** Mark, who frequently hosted dinner parties, often found his fridge overflowing with forgotten leftovers. After decluttering and organizing his fridge, he was able to store ingredients more efficiently and reduce food waste.

**The Living Room: Space for Connection**

The living room is where families relax, entertain, and connect. However, it can easily become a dumping ground for miscellaneous items, from remote controls to magazines and toys. A clutter-free living room promotes relaxation and fosters a welcoming atmosphere for guests.

**Step 1: Tackle the Electronics** Living rooms often house TVs, gaming systems, and a plethora of remotes and chargers. Start by decluttering outdated electronics and storing what remains in an organized manner.

**Practical Tip:** Use a media console with closed storage to hide unsightly cables and electronics. Consider a universal remote to reduce the number of remotes cluttering the coffee table. Label cords and chargers to avoid confusion.

**Story Example:** Emily's living room was dominated by a tangle of cables and remotes, making it difficult to enjoy movie nights with her family. After investing in a media console and a universal remote, her living room became a more relaxing and organized space.

**Step 2: Streamline Décor and Furniture** Too many decorative items and furniture pieces can make a living room feel cramped. Keep only the items that you love and that contribute to the room's ambiance.

**Practical Tip:** Choose a few key pieces of décor that align with your style, and eliminate the rest. Arrange furniture to create an open, inviting layout that facilitates conversation. Consider multifunctional furniture, like ottomans with storage, to reduce clutter.

**Story Example:** Laura's living room was filled with mismatched furniture and knick-knacks, making it feel cluttered. After decluttering and rearranging the furniture, she created a more cohesive and comfortable space where her family loved to gather.

**Step 3: Create Functional Zones** A well-organized living room has designated areas for different activities, such as reading, watching TV, and socializing. Define these zones to make the space more functional.

**Practical Tip:** Use area rugs or furniture placement to delineate different zones. For example, place a comfortable chair and a lamp in a corner to create a cozy reading nook. Keep a basket for remotes and magazines to maintain order.

**Story Example:** David used to struggle with a living room that doubled as his home office, resulting in clutter everywhere. By creating distinct zones for work and relaxation, he was able to keep his workspace tidy and enjoy a clutter-free environment after hours.

## The Bedroom: Your Personal Retreat

The bedroom should be a sanctuary for rest and relaxation, but clutter can quickly turn it into a source of stress. By decluttering your bedroom, you can create a peaceful environment that promotes better sleep and relaxation.

**Step 1: Declutter the Wardrobe** Clothing is one of the biggest sources of bedroom clutter. Start by sorting through your wardrobe, keeping only what you wear and love.

**Practical Tip:** Use the "one-year rule"—if you haven't worn it in a year, it's time to let it go. Organize your closet by category (e.g., shirts, pants, dresses) and color to make getting dressed easier. Consider seasonal rotation, storing off-season clothes out of sight.

**Story Example:** Jennifer had a closet overflowing with clothes, yet she struggled to find outfits she liked. After decluttering and organizing her wardrobe, she found it easier to get dressed in the morning and felt more confident in her clothing choices.

**Step 2: Simplify Bedside Tables** Nightstands often become catch-alls for books, chargers, and random items. Clear them off to create a more serene sleeping environment.

**Practical Tip:** Keep only the essentials on your bedside table—a lamp, a book, and perhaps a glass of water. Use a drawer organizer to keep smaller items like chargers and lip balm neatly stored away.

**Story Example:** Michael's bedside table was piled high with old magazines, unused chargers, and other clutter. After simplifying it, he found that his bedroom felt more peaceful and he slept better.

**Step 3: Create a Calm Atmosphere** Your bedroom should evoke calmness and relaxation. Declutter the room and introduce elements that promote tranquillity.

**Practical Tip:** Remove unnecessary furniture and décor that don't contribute to a restful environment. Choose soothing colours, soft lighting, and cozy textiles. Consider a sound machine or blackout curtains to enhance sleep quality.

**Story Example:** After decluttering her bedroom, including removing a bulky dresser that dominated the space, Rachel introduced soft lighting and neutral tones. The result was a calming retreat that helped her unwind at the end of the day.

## The Bathroom: A Place for Relaxation

The bathroom is where you start and end your day, making it essential for it to be a clutter-free zone. A clean, organized bathroom contributes to a sense of calm and helps streamline your daily routines.

**Step 1: Clear Out Unused Toiletries** Many bathrooms are cluttered with expired or unused toiletries. Go through your cabinets and drawers, discarding anything that's no longer needed.

**Practical Tip:** Limit your toiletries to daily essentials. Use drawer dividers or baskets to organize items by category (e.g., skincare, haircare). Store bulk items in a linen closet or under the sink to keep the space uncluttered.

**Story Example:** Lisa found that her bathroom drawers were filled with half-used bottles of lotion and expired makeup. After decluttering, she streamlined her routine and made her bathroom a more pleasant place to get ready each day.

**Step 2: Organize Towels and Linens** Towels and linens can take up valuable space if not stored properly. Keep your bathroom organized by managing these essentials effectively.

**Practical Tip:** Roll towels and store them in a basket or on a shelf for easy access. Limit the number of towels and linens to what you actually use. If space allows, consider a linen closet nearby to store extras.

**Story Example:** Maria had a habit of collecting towels, leading to a cluttered bathroom. After decluttering and organizing her towels, she found that her bathroom looked more spacious and was easier to clean.

**Step 3: Maintain a Clean, Clutter-Free Space** A clutter-free bathroom requires regular maintenance. Develop simple habits to keep it clean and organized.

**Practical Tip:** Wipe down surfaces daily and do a quick declutter once a week. Keep cleaning supplies within reach to make it easier to maintain a spotless bathroom.

**Story Example:** John found that his bathroom quickly became cluttered again after he cleaned it. By adopting a routine of daily maintenance and weekly deep cleaning, he was able to keep it looking tidy and inviting.

# Section 2: Building Functional Storage Systems

Creating a clutter-free home is not just about getting rid of things; it's also about finding the right place for what you choose to keep. Functional storage systems play a crucial role in maintaining an organized and serene environment. In this section, we'll explore how to choose the right storage solutions, maximize space efficiency, and maintain order to prevent future clutter.

## Choosing the Right Storage Solutions

Selecting the right storage solutions is the foundation of an organized home. The goal is to create systems that are both functional and aesthetically pleasing, making it easier to keep your space tidy.

## Step 1: Assess Your Storage Needs

Before purchasing storage solutions, it's essential to assess your specific needs. Consider the type and quantity of items you need to store, the available space, and how you use each room.

**Practical Tip:** Start by taking inventory of your belongings. For example, if you have a large collection of books, you'll need sturdy shelves. If your wardrobe is overflowing, consider adding more hanging space or drawer organizers. Think about how often you use certain items and prioritize storage solutions that offer easy access for frequently used items.

**Story Example:** Emily had always struggled with organizing her home office. She had stacks of papers, books, and office supplies scattered everywhere. After assessing her needs, she realized that her current storage wasn't adequate. She invested in a filing cabinet for paperwork, wall-mounted shelves for books, and drawer organizers for supplies. This transformation made her workspace more functional and enjoyable.

## Step 2: Consider the Space and Style

Storage solutions should complement the style and function of each room. The key is to find a balance between practicality and aesthetics.

**Practical Tip:** Choose storage solutions that blend seamlessly with your décor. For example, opt for woven baskets in a living room with a rustic feel or sleek, modern storage units for a minimalist space. Furniture with built-in storage, like ottomans or coffee tables with hidden compartments, can help keep your home organized without sacrificing style.

**Story Example:** Sarah's small apartment had limited storage space, and she struggled with keeping her living room tidy. She chose a sofa with built-in storage and added a coffee table with drawers. These stylish, space-saving solutions allowed her to store blankets, remote controls, and magazines out of sight, giving her living room a clean and cohesive look.

## Step 3: Prioritize Functionality

While aesthetics is important, functionality should be the top priority when selecting storage solutions. Consider how easily you can access and maintain your storage.

**Practical Tip:** opt for open shelving or clear containers in spaces like the kitchen or pantry, where quick access is essential. In the bedroom, consider under-bed storage for off-season clothing or bedding. In the bathroom, use tiered shelves or wall-mounted organizers to keep toiletries within reach without cluttering countertops.

**Story Example:** Mark found that his bathroom countertop was constantly cluttered with toiletries, making it difficult to keep clean. He installed a wall-mounted organizer and a tiered shelf to store items like toothpaste, soap, and skincare products. This small change made his morning routine smoother and kept his bathroom looking neat.

## Maximizing Space Efficiency

Even in the smallest of spaces, there are ways to maximize storage efficiency. By thinking creatively and utilizing every inch of available space, you can make your home more functional and less cluttered.

## Step 1: Utilize Vertical Space

Vertical space is often underutilized in homes. By going vertical, you can free up floor space and create additional storage.

**Practical Tip:** Install shelves, hooks, or pegboards on walls to store items like books, kitchen utensils, or tools. In closets, use vertical shoe racks or hanging organizers to maximize space. Consider adding shelves above doorways or in corners to store items that are used less frequently.

**Story Example:** Jessica's kitchen had limited cabinet space, and she often struggled to find room for all her cooking supplies. She installed a pegboard on the wall above her counter, where she hung pots, pans, and utensils. This solution not only saved cabinet space but also added a decorative element to her kitchen.

## Step 2: Make Use of Hidden Spaces

Hidden spaces, such as under beds, behind doors, or inside furniture, offer valuable storage opportunities that are often overlooked.

**Practical Tip:** Use under-bed storage containers for items like shoes, seasonal clothing, or extra bedding. Install hooks or racks behind doors to hang coats, bags, or accessories. Opt for furniture with hidden storage compartments, like beds with built-in drawers or benches with lift-up seats.

**Story Example:** Maria lived in a small studio apartment and struggled with finding space for her belongings. She invested in a bed with built-in drawers, where she stored her extra linens and winter clothes. She also added hooks behind her closet door for bags and scarves. These hidden storage solutions helped her keep her small space organized and clutter-free.

## Step 3: Maximize Closet Space

Closets are prime real estate for storage, but they're often underutilized or poorly organized. Maximizing closet space can significantly reduce clutter in your home.

**Practical Tip:** Use double-hang rods to create additional hanging space for clothes. Add shelves or cubbies for shoes, bags, and accessories. Use slim, uniform hangers to save space and keep your closet looking neat. Consider adding a closet organizer system to make the most of every inch.

**Story Example:** Daniel had a walk-in closet, but it was always a mess, and he struggled to find what he needed. He installed a closet organizer with double-hang rods, shelves, and drawers. This allowed him to store his clothes, shoes, and accessories more efficiently, and he was able to keep his closet tidy and accessible.

## Maintaining Order and Preventing Future Clutter

Once you've decluttered and organized your home, the next challenge is maintaining that order. Developing habits and systems to prevent future clutter is key to ensuring your home remains a sanctuary.

## Step 1: Establish Daily and Weekly Routines

Regular maintenance is essential to prevent clutter from accumulating again. Establishing simple daily and weekly routines can help keep your home organized.

**Practical Tip:** Spend 10-15 minutes each day tidying up high-traffic areas like the kitchen and living room. Make it a habit to put things back where they belong after use. Set aside time each week to declutter and reorganize one area of your home, such as a drawer, closet, or countertop.

**Story Example:** Rachel used to spend hours on weekends cleaning her house, only to have it become cluttered again by the middle of the week. She started incorporating daily tidying into her routine, spending a few minutes each evening putting things away and wiping down surfaces. This small change helped her maintain a clutter-free home without feeling overwhelmed.

## Step 2: Implement the One-In, One-Out Rule

The one-in, one-out rule is a simple but effective way to prevent clutter from returning. For every new item you bring into your home, something else must go.

**Practical Tip:** Before buying something new, consider what you already have and whether you truly need it. If you bring in a new piece of clothing, donate or discard an old one. Apply this rule to all areas of your home, including kitchen gadgets, books, and décor.

**Story Example:** Lisa had a habit of buying new kitchen gadgets, which led to overcrowded drawers and cabinets. She started following the one-in, one-out rule, which helped her control her impulse purchases and maintain an organized kitchen. Now, when she buys a new gadget, she makes sure to donate an older one that she no longer uses.

## Step 3: Manage Incoming Items

One of the biggest challenges to maintaining a clutter-free home is managing the constant influx of new items, such as mail, packages, and gifts. Having a system in place to handle these items can help prevent clutter from accumulating.

**Practical Tip:** Designate a specific spot for incoming items, such as a basket for mail or a table for packages. Sort through these items regularly, and make decisions about what to keep, discard, or file away. Create a system for managing paper clutter, such as scanning important documents and shredding what you don't need.

**Story Example:** John often found his dining table covered in mail, bills, and packages, making it difficult to enjoy meals with his family. He designated a basket by the front door for incoming mail and set up a small filing system for important documents. This helped him manage the flow of items into his home and keep his dining area clutter-free.

## Step 4: Cultivate Mindfulness About Your Space

Mindfulness plays a significant role in maintaining an organized home. Being intentional about what you bring into your space and how you use it can help you avoid unnecessary clutter.

**Practical Tip:** Regularly assess your belongings and your space to ensure that everything serves a purpose and brings you joy. Practice gratitude for what you have and resist the urge to accumulate more. Consider the environmental impact of your purchases and how they align with your values.

**Story Example:** Emma started practicing mindfulness after noticing that her home was filling up with items she didn't really need or love. She began to carefully consider each purchase and how it would fit into her home and her life. This shift in mindset helped her maintain a clutter-free home that truly reflected her values and lifestyle.

# Section 3: Personalizing Your Space—Making Your Home a Sanctuary

Creating a home that truly feels like a sanctuary is about more than just removing clutter; it's about infusing your space with personality, purpose, and peace. This section will guide you through the process of personalizing your space, creating zones for relaxation and productivity, and sustaining a sanctuary mindset to ensure your home remains a haven.

## Infusing Personality into Your Home

Your home should be a reflection of who you are, your values, and your experiences. Personalizing your space is about bringing your unique personality into every corner, making your home a place where you feel truly comfortable and at ease.

## Step 1: Displaying Meaningful Items

One of the simplest ways to infuse personality into your home is by displaying items that hold personal significance. These could be family heirlooms, travel souvenirs, or pieces of art that speak to your soul.

**Practical Tip:** Choose a few meaningful items to display prominently in your home. For example, you might create a gallery wall of family photos in the living room or display souvenirs from your travels on a shelf in the bedroom. The key is to curate these items so that they don't overwhelm the space but rather enhance its character.

**Story Example:** Mary loved to travel, and over the years, she had collected various souvenirs from around the world. However, they were scattered throughout her home, making her space feel cluttered. She decided to create a dedicated travel corner in her living room, where she arranged her favourite souvenirs on a stylish shelf and hung a world map on the wall. This not only personalized her space but also sparked joy every time she walked by.

## Step 2: Choosing Colors and Textures That Reflect You

Colors and textures play a significant role in the ambiance of your home. Choosing the right palette can make your space feel more inviting and reflective of your personality.

**Practical Tip:** Start by identifying the colors and textures that resonate with you. If you love the ocean, consider incorporating shades of blue and green with natural textures like wood and linen. If you're drawn to warmth and coziness, opt for earthy tones and soft, plush fabrics. Use these elements in your décor, such as through throw pillows, rugs, curtains, and wall art.

**Story Example:** Karen had always loved the beach, but her city apartment felt far removed from the calming shores she adored. She decided to bring the beach into her home by painting her walls a soft seafoam green and adding coastal-inspired décor like driftwood accents, woven baskets, and linen curtains. The transformation made her apartment feel like a personal retreat, reminding her of the places she loved most.

## Step 3: Incorporating Your Hobbies and Passions

Your home should be a space where you can indulge in your hobbies and passions. Incorporating these into your décor and layout can make your home feel more uniquely yours.

**Practical Tip:** Dedicate a specific area of your home to your hobbies. For example, if you love reading, create a cozy reading nook with a comfortable chair, good lighting, and a bookshelf filled with your favorite titles. If you're an artist, set up a small studio space where you can paint or craft. These personalized areas will make your home more functional and enjoyable.

**Story Example:** Tom was an avid musician, but his guitar and piano were often shoved into corners of his home, unused and neglected. He decided to create a music corner in his living room, where he placed his instruments, a comfortable chair, and a few pieces of music-themed art. This not only made his home feel more personal but also encouraged him to play music more often, bringing joy and relaxation into his daily life.

## Creating Zones for Relaxation and Productivity

In today's busy world, it's essential to have spaces in your home dedicated to both relaxation and productivity. These zones can help you unwind after a long day or stay focused when you need to get things done.

## Step 1: Designing a Relaxation Zone

Your home should include at least one area specifically designed for relaxation. This is where you can retreat to unwind, read a book, meditate, or simply enjoy some quiet time.

**Practical Tip:** Choose a spot in your home that feels calm and secluded, whether it's a corner of your living room, a cozy nook in your bedroom, or even a spot in your backyard. Furnish it with comfortable seating, soft lighting, and calming colors. Consider adding elements like candles, plants, or a sound machine to enhance the peaceful atmosphere.

**Story Example:** Rebecca found it challenging to relax in her busy household, with kids, pets, and a never-ending to-do list. She decided to transform a small corner of her bedroom into a relaxation zone. She added a comfy armchair, a small table for her tea, and a shelf with her favourite books. This became her go-to spot for unwinding at the end of the day, helping her to feel more centered and at peace.

## Step 2: Setting Up a Productivity Zone

Just as important as having a place to relax is having a designated area where you can focus and be productive. Whether you work from home, study, or manage household tasks, a productivity zone can help you stay organized and efficient.

**Practical Tip:** Choose a quiet, well-lit area for your productivity zone. This could be a home office, a desk in the living room, or even a designated section of the kitchen. Equip it with everything you need to stay focused, such as a comfortable chair, a good desk, and proper lighting. Keep the space free from distractions and clutter, and personalize it with items that motivate you, like a vision board or inspirational quotes.

**Story Example:** John often found himself distracted while working from home, which affected his productivity. He decided to set up a dedicated home office in a spare bedroom. He invested in a sturdy desk, an ergonomic chair, and some motivational wall art. By keeping this area clutter-free and focused, John was able to increase his productivity and separate work from the rest of his home life.

## Step 3: Balancing the Two Zones

Balancing relaxation and productivity zones in your home is key to maintaining a harmonious environment. These areas should complement each other, allowing you to switch between work and rest with ease.

**Practical Tip:** If space is limited, consider creating multifunctional zones. For example, a corner of your living room can serve as both a reading nook and a home office, depending on your needs at the time. Use storage solutions, like baskets or bins, to quickly transition the space from work mode to relaxation mode. The goal is to make these transitions seamless so that you can maintain a healthy balance between work and rest.

**Story Example:** Angela lived in a small studio apartment, where space was at a premium. She cleverly divided her living area into a multifunctional zone, using a bookshelf as a divider. On one side, she set up a small desk for work, and on the other, she created a cozy seating area for relaxation. By using the bookshelf to store work-related items, she could easily switch the space from a home office to a lounge area, helping her maintain a balance between productivity and relaxation.

**Sustaining a Sanctuary Mindset**

Creating a sanctuary in your home is not a one-time project; it's an ongoing mindset. Maintaining this mindset involves nurturing your space and yourself, ensuring that your home continues to be a place of peace and rejuvenation.

## Step 1: Regularly Refreshing Your Space

Even the most beautifully curated spaces can start to feel stale over time. Regularly refreshing your space helps keep it feeling vibrant and welcoming.

**Practical Tip:** Make it a habit to periodically assess your home and make small updates. This could be as simple as rearranging furniture, adding a new piece of art, or changing out throw pillows. Seasonal changes, like switching from summer to winter décor, can also help keep your home feeling fresh and aligned with the time of year.

**Story Example:** Every spring, Laura liked to give her living room a little refresh. She would swap out heavy blankets and dark-coloured decor for lighter fabrics and brighter colours. This simple change made her space feel renewed and ready for the warmer months, helping her stay connected to the changing seasons.

## Step 2: Mindful Consumption

Part of sustaining a sanctuary mindset is being mindful about what you bring into your home. Each item should add value, whether through functionality, beauty, or emotional significance.

**Practical Tip:** Before making a purchase, ask yourself if the item will enhance your home or if it might contribute to future clutter. Consider its purpose, where it will go, and how it aligns with your overall vision for your space. By being selective, you can maintain the tranquility of your home and avoid the accumulation of unnecessary items.

**Story Example:** David used to buy home décor on impulse, which led to a cluttered and disjointed space. After decluttering, he adopted a more mindful approach, carefully considering each purchase. This new mindset helped him create a cohesive and serene environment that truly reflected his style and values.

## Step 3: Nurturing Yourself and Your Space

A sanctuary mindset isn't just about maintaining your physical space; it's also about nurturing yourself. Your home should be a place where you can recharge and take care of your well-being.

**Practical Tip:** Create rituals that help you feel connected to your home and yourself. This could be a morning routine that includes opening the windows to let in fresh air, lighting a candle during evening relaxation, or practicing gratitude for your space. These small acts of self-care can enhance your connection to your home and ensure it remains a sanctuary.

**Story Example:** Emily started a daily ritual of spending a few minutes in her relaxation zone each morning, sipping tea and practicing mindfulness. This simple routine helped her start her day with a sense of calm and gratitude, reinforcing her home as a place of peace and renewal

# Chapter 4: Decluttering Your Mind—Clearing Mental Clutter

# Section 1: Identifying Sources of Mental Clutter

Mental clutter is the unseen weight that often holds us back from living fully in the present. Just as physical clutter can overwhelm a space, mental clutter can overwhelm our minds, leading to stress, anxiety, and a lack of focus. The first step in clearing this clutter is to identify its sources. In this section, we'll explore the various forms of mental clutter, from information overload to unresolved emotions, and provide practical advice on how to recognize and begin to address them.

**Information Overload: Too Much to Process**

In the digital age, we are constantly bombarded with information. From news updates and social media feeds to endless emails and notifications, our brains are inundated with more data than ever before. This constant influx of information can lead to what is known as "information overload," where our minds become overwhelmed by the sheer volume of data we are trying to process.

**Practical Advice:** One of the most effective ways to combat information overload is to set boundaries around your information consumption. Start by identifying the most essential sources of information in your life—whether it's the news, work-related emails, or social media—and prioritize these over less important or non-essential sources. For example, you might decide to limit your news intake to just 15 minutes a day or unsubscribe from email lists that no longer serve you.

Another strategy is to schedule specific times for checking emails and social media rather than allowing these tasks to interrupt your day. By compartmentalizing your information intake, you can prevent your brain from becoming overwhelmed and allow yourself more mental space to focus on what truly matters.

**Story Example:** Consider the experience of Sarah, a marketing manager who found herself constantly distracted by her phone. Every few minutes, she would receive notifications from social media, news apps, and work emails, making it difficult for her to concentrate on her tasks. Realizing that this was contributing to her stress, Sarah decided to turn off non-essential notifications and set specific times in the day to check her phone. This simple change helped her regain control over her time and reduced the mental clutter that had been clouding her mind.

## Unresolved Emotions: The Weight of the Past

Unresolved emotions are another significant source of mental clutter. Whether it's lingering guilt, unresolved conflicts, or unprocessed grief, these emotions can occupy a large portion of our mental space, often without us even realizing it. They manifest as intrusive thoughts, emotional outbursts, or a general sense of unease, preventing us from fully engaging in the present.

**Practical Advice:** To begin clearing this type of mental clutter, it's important to acknowledge and process these unresolved emotions. One effective method is journaling. Writing about your feelings can help you gain clarity and insight into what's been weighing on your mind. Consider setting aside time each day or week to journal about any unresolved emotions or experiences that continue to affect you.

Another approach is to seek professional support, such as therapy or counselling. Talking through your emotions with a trained professional can help you process them in a healthy way, allowing you to move forward without the burden of unresolved issues. It's also helpful to practice mindfulness techniques, such as meditation, to stay present and prevent your mind from dwelling on the past.

**Story Example:** David had been carrying the weight of a falling out with a close friend for years. Though they hadn't spoken in a long time, the unresolved anger and sadness would frequently surface in his thoughts, affecting his mood and concentration. After some reflection, David decided to start journaling about the incident. Over time, he gained a better understanding of his feelings and even reached out to his friend to make amends. While the friendship didn't fully repair, the act of addressing the unresolved emotions lifted a significant mental burden, allowing David to focus more on his current relationships.

## Negative Thinking Patterns: The Mental Noise

Negative thinking patterns are another common source of mental clutter. These patterns often manifest as self-doubt, catastrophizing, or perfectionism, and can be incredibly draining. They create a mental noise that drowns out positive thoughts and can lead to feelings of anxiety, depression, and a lack of self-worth.

**Practical Advice:** The first step in addressing negative thinking patterns is to become aware of them. Pay attention to the thoughts that frequently run through your mind. Are they overly critical or pessimistic? Do you often jump to worst-case scenarios or set unrealistically high standards for yourself?

Once you've identified these patterns, challenge them. Ask yourself whether these thoughts are based on facts or assumptions. Often, negative thinking is rooted in irrational beliefs or fears. Cognitive-behavioural techniques, such as reframing, can be helpful in this process. For example, if you catch yourself thinking, "I'm never going to succeed at this," try reframing it to, "I may face challenges, but I have the skills and determination to overcome them."

In addition to cognitive strategies, it's important to cultivate a positive mindset through gratitude and self-compassion. Take time each day to reflect on what you're grateful for, and practice being kind to yourself, especially when you make mistakes.

**Story Example:** Emily was a talented graphic designer, but she often struggled with perfectionism. She would spend hours tweaking her designs, unable to accept that they were good enough. This negative thinking pattern not only caused her stress but also slowed her productivity. After recognizing this pattern, Emily started using cognitive-behavioural techniques to challenge her perfectionistic thoughts. She began setting time limits on her projects and reminding herself that "done is better than perfect." Over time, she noticed a significant decrease in her stress levels and an improvement in her overall well-being.

## External Pressures: The Burden of Expectations

External pressures, such as societal expectations, family obligations, and work demands, can also contribute to mental clutter. These pressures often manifest as an internal dialogue of "shoulds" and "musts," leaving little room for personal desires and needs. The result is a cluttered mind filled with stress and anxiety over meeting these expectations.

**Practical Advice:** To manage external pressures, it's essential to establish boundaries and prioritize your own well-being. Start by identifying the sources of pressure in your life. Are you constantly trying to meet someone else's expectations? Are you taking on more responsibilities than you can handle?

Once you've identified these pressures, practice saying "no" when necessary. This might mean turning down extra work assignments, setting limits with family members, or choosing not to engage in activities that don't align with your values. It's also important to regularly check in with yourself to ensure that you're not overcommitting or sacrificing your own needs for the sake of others.

Another effective strategy is to redefine success on your terms. Instead of trying to meet society's or others' expectations, focus on what success means to you personally. This shift in perspective can help reduce the mental clutter associated with trying to live up to external standards.

**Story Example:** Linda was a mother of two and a full-time teacher, constantly juggling the demands of work and family. She often felt overwhelmed by the pressure to be the perfect mom, wife, and employee. After a particularly stressful week, Linda realized that she was trying to meet everyone else's expectations while neglecting her own needs. She decided to set boundaries at work, saying no to extra assignments that weren't essential. At home, she simplified her routine and started setting aside time for self-care. These changes allowed Linda to reduce the mental clutter caused by external pressures and focus more on her well-being.

## Unfinished Tasks: The Mental To-Do List

Unfinished tasks, whether they are related to work, home, or personal projects, can create a mental to-do list that lingers in your mind, contributing to stress and mental clutter. These tasks often weigh on you, making it difficult to fully relax or focus on the present moment.

**Practical Advice:** To address the mental clutter caused by unfinished tasks, it's important to create a clear and manageable to-do list. Start by writing down all the tasks that are occupying your mind. Then, prioritize them based on urgency and importance. Break down larger tasks into smaller, more manageable steps, and set deadlines for each step.

Another effective strategy is to adopt the "two-minute rule." If a task can be completed in two minutes or less, do it immediately rather than adding it to your to-do list. This approach can help you quickly clear smaller tasks from your mind, reducing the overall mental load.

It's also helpful to regularly review and update your to-do list. Remove tasks that are no longer relevant or important, and celebrate your accomplishments by checking off completed tasks. This practice can help you maintain a sense of progress and reduce the mental clutter associated with unfinished tasks.

**Story Example:** Mark had a habit of mentally keeping track of all his unfinished tasks, from work projects to household chores. This mental list often kept him up at night, causing stress and anxiety. After learning about the two-minute rule, Mark started tackling small tasks immediately instead of letting them accumulate. He also began keeping a physical to-do list, which helped him organize his tasks and reduce the mental burden of trying to remember everything. As a result, Mark experienced a noticeable decrease in stress and an increase in productivity.

# Section 2: Techniques for Mental Decluttering

Mental clutter can be just as overwhelming and debilitating as physical clutter, but unlike a messy room, it's not always easy to recognize or address. However, by using effective techniques for mental decluttering, you can create a clearer, more focused mind. This section will explore practical strategies to help you declutter your mind, supported by real-world examples and stories that illustrate their impact.

## 1. Mindfulness: Being Present in the Moment

Mindfulness is one of the most powerful techniques for mental decluttering. It involves paying attention to the present moment without judgment, allowing you to clear your mind of unnecessary thoughts and worries. By practicing mindfulness, you can reduce stress, improve focus, and create mental space for more important things.

**Practical Advice:** Begin by incorporating mindfulness into your daily routine. You don't need to set aside hours each day; even a few minutes can make a significant difference. Start with simple breathing exercises: find a quiet place, sit comfortably, and focus on your breath. Notice the sensation of the air entering and leaving your lungs. If your mind starts to wander, gently bring your attention back to your breath.

Another effective way to practice mindfulness is through mindful walking. As you walk, pay attention to each step, the feel of the ground beneath your feet, and the sights and sounds around you. This practice can help ground you in the present moment, reducing mental clutter.

**Story Example:** Jessica, a busy mother of three, found herself constantly overwhelmed by the demands of her day-to-day life. Her mind was always racing with thoughts of what needed to be done, leaving her feeling anxious and stressed. After attending a mindfulness workshop, she started practicing mindful breathing for five minutes each morning. Over time, she noticed a significant reduction in her anxiety levels. She felt more present with her children and better equipped to handle the challenges of her day. By focusing on the present moment, Jessica was able to clear her mind and find peace amidst the chaos.

## 2. Journaling: Clearing Your Mind on Paper

Journaling is another highly effective technique for mental decluttering. By writing down your thoughts, you can transfer them from your mind to paper, freeing up mental space and gaining clarity on issues that may be bothering you. Journaling can help you process emotions, organize your thoughts, and identify patterns in your thinking that contribute to mental clutter.

**Practical Advice:** Set aside time each day or week to journal, even if it's just for a few minutes. You don't need to write in a structured way—just let your thoughts flow freely onto the page. Consider starting with a brain dump: write down everything that's on your mind, no matter how trivial it may seem. This practice can help you clear out the mental clutter and focus on what truly matters.

If you're dealing with specific challenges, try journaling about those. Ask yourself questions like, "What's really bothering me about this situation?" or "What can I do to move forward?" Writing about your feelings and thoughts can provide valuable insights and help you see things from a new perspective.

**Story Example:** Michael, a project manager, was struggling to keep up with the demands of his job. He often felt overwhelmed by the number of tasks on his to-do list, and his mind was constantly racing with thoughts of what needed to be done. A colleague suggested he try journaling to clear his mind. Michael began writing in a journal each night, focusing on the challenges he faced that day and how he felt about them. This practice helped him gain clarity on his priorities and allowed him to approach his work with a clearer, more focused mind. Over time, he found that journaling not only reduced his stress but also improved his productivity.

## 3. Meditation: Finding Inner Peace

Meditation is a practice that has been used for centuries to quiet the mind and find inner peace. By meditating regularly, you can reduce mental clutter, improve your ability to concentrate, and develop a greater sense of calm and clarity. Meditation helps you detach from the constant stream of thoughts that can overwhelm your mind, allowing you to focus on the present moment and experience a sense of mental freedom.

**Practical Advice:** Start with short meditation sessions, especially if you're new to the practice. Find a quiet place where you won't be disturbed, sit comfortably, and close your eyes. Focus on your breath, a mantra, or a specific point in your body. If your mind starts to wander, gently bring your attention back to your focal point.

As you become more comfortable with meditation, you can gradually increase the length of your sessions. There are also various types of meditation you can explore, such as guided meditation, loving-kindness meditation, and body scan meditation. Experiment with different methods to find what works best for you.

**Story Example:** Emily, a nurse working long shifts in a busy hospital, often found herself mentally exhausted by the end of the day. The constant demands of her job left little room for relaxation, and her mind was always cluttered with thoughts of patients, procedures, and paperwork. A friend recommended meditation as a way to unwind and clear her mind. Emily started meditating for just five minutes each night before bed, focusing on her breath and letting go of the day's stresses. This simple practice helped her find a sense of calm and clarity, allowing her to sleep better and wake up feeling refreshed. Meditation became an essential tool for managing her mental clutter and maintaining her well-being.

## 4. Setting Boundaries: Protecting Your Mental Space

Mental clutter can often result from a lack of boundaries, whether it's saying yes to too many commitments, allowing others to dictate your time, or being constantly available to others. Setting boundaries is crucial for protecting your mental space and preventing overwhelm.

**Practical Advice:** Start by identifying areas in your life where you feel overextended or overwhelmed. Are there tasks or commitments you've taken on that aren't serving you? Are you allowing others to encroach on your time or energy?

Once you've identified these areas, practice saying no when necessary. This doesn't mean you have to turn down every request, but it's important to prioritize your well-being and only take on what you can handle. Communicate your boundaries clearly to others, and don't be afraid to enforce them. For example, if you need uninterrupted time to focus on a project, let your colleagues or family members know that you'll be unavailable during certain hours.

**Story Example:** Rachel, a freelance graphic designer, often found herself overwhelmed by the demands of her clients. She had a hard time saying no to new projects, even when her schedule was already full. This led to long hours, stress, and a constant feeling of mental clutter. After a particularly stressful week, Rachel realized she needed to set boundaries to protect her mental space. She started by setting clear working hours and communicating them to her clients. She also became more selective about the projects she took on, only accepting work that aligned with her goals and values. These changes allowed Rachel to regain control over her time and mental energy, reducing her stress and improving her overall quality of life.

## 5. Prioritizing and Organizing: Streamlining Your Mental Load

Another effective technique for mental decluttering is prioritizing and organizing your thoughts and tasks. When your mind is cluttered with too many to-dos, it can be difficult to focus on what's truly important. By prioritizing your tasks and organizing your thoughts, you can reduce mental clutter and increase your efficiency.

**Practical Advice:** Start by making a list of everything you need to do, then prioritize the tasks based on urgency and importance. Use tools like to-do lists, calendars, or project management apps to keep track of your tasks and deadlines. Breaking down larger tasks into smaller, more manageable steps can also make them feel less overwhelming.

Another helpful strategy is to practice time blocking, where you allocate specific blocks of time for different tasks or activities. This approach can help you focus on one task at a time, reducing the mental clutter that comes from trying to juggle multiple things at once.

**Story Example:** Tom, a sales executive, was constantly juggling multiple tasks and projects at work. His mind was always racing with thoughts of what needed to be done, and he often felt overwhelmed by his workload. After attending a time management workshop, Tom began prioritizing his tasks each morning and using time blocking to structure his day. This approach helped him focus on one task at a time and reduced the mental clutter that had been causing him stress. As a result, Tom became more productive and found that he had more mental energy to devote to both his work and personal life.

## 6. Digital Detox: Reducing Screen Time and Information Overload

In today's digital world, it's easy to become overwhelmed by the constant stream of information coming from our screens. Whether it's social media, emails, or news updates, digital clutter can contribute significantly to mental clutter. A digital detox can help reduce this overload and create more mental space.

**Practical Advice:** Start by setting limits on your screen time, especially for non-essential activities like social media or browsing the web. You can use apps or built-in features on your devices to monitor and control your usage. Consider designating specific times of the day when you'll unplug from your devices, such as during meals, before bed, or during family time.

Another effective strategy is to declutter your digital space. Unsubscribe from email lists you no longer need, delete apps that you don't use, and organize your files and folders. By creating a more organized and intentional digital environment, you can reduce the mental clutter associated with digital overload.

**Story Example:** Kevin, a software engineer, realized that he was spending far too much time on his phone, especially on social media. This constant screen time was contributing to his feelings of anxiety and distraction. To combat this, Kevin decided to do a digital detox. He started by setting limits on his social media usage and designated tech-free times in his day. He also decluttered his digital space, unsubscribing from unnecessary email lists and organizing his files. These changes helped Kevin reduce his mental clutter, allowing him to focus better on his work and enjoy more meaningful offline activities.

# Section 3: Maintaining Mental Clarity

Achieving mental clarity is one thing, but maintaining it over time is an ongoing process. Just as a clean home can become cluttered again without regular upkeep, mental clarity requires consistent effort to preserve. In this section, we'll explore practical strategies for sustaining mental clarity in your daily life. These approaches will help you navigate the inevitable challenges and distractions that can cloud your mind, keeping you focused and centered. Through real-world examples and actionable advice, you'll discover how to maintain a clear and peaceful mind in the long term.

## 1. Establishing Daily Routines for Mental Clarity

One of the most effective ways to maintain mental clarity is by establishing daily routines that support your mental well-being. Routines create structure in your life, helping you stay organized and focused. By integrating practices that promote mental clarity into your daily schedule, you can prevent mental clutter from building up.

**Practical Advice:** Start by creating a morning routine that sets a positive tone for the day. This might include practices like meditation, journaling, or a short exercise session.

These activities help clear your mind, boost your mood, and prepare you for the day ahead.

For example, you could begin your day with a few minutes of mindful breathing or meditation. This simple practice helps to center your mind, allowing you to approach the day with a calm and clear mindset. Follow this with journaling to organize your thoughts and set your intentions for the day. Writing down your goals and priorities can help you stay focused and avoid mental clutter throughout the day.

**Story Example:** Sarah, a busy marketing executive, used to start her days in a rush, checking emails and diving straight into work. This often left her feeling scattered and overwhelmed by midday. Realizing she needed a change, Sarah decided to implement a morning routine. She started waking up 30 minutes earlier to meditate, journal, and plan her day. Over time, this routine became a non-negotiable part of her life. The impact was profound—Sarah found herself more focused, less stressed, and better equipped to handle the demands of her job. Her morning routine became the foundation for maintaining mental clarity throughout the day.

In addition to your morning routine, consider establishing an evening routine that helps you unwind and prepare for a restful night's sleep. This might include activities like reading, reflecting on your day, or practicing gratitude. A consistent evening routine can help you clear your mind of the day's stresses, promoting better sleep and mental clarity for the following day.

## 2. Practicing Gratitude: Shifting Your Focus to the Positive

Gratitude is a powerful tool for maintaining mental clarity. When you focus on what you're grateful for, you shift your attention away from negative thoughts and worries, which can contribute to mental clutter. By regularly practicing gratitude, you can cultivate a more positive mindset and maintain a clearer, more focused mind.

**Practical Advice:** Incorporate gratitude into your daily routine by keeping a gratitude journal. Each day, write down three things you're grateful for, no matter how small they may seem. This practice can help you develop a habit of focusing on the positive aspects of your life, reducing the mental clutter associated with negative thinking.

Another way to practice gratitude is by expressing it to others. Take the time to thank the people in your life for their support, kindness, or simply for being there. This not only strengthens your relationships but also reinforces a positive mindset that contributes to mental clarity.

**Story Example:** David, a teacher, struggled with anxiety and negative thoughts that often clouded his mind. After reading about the benefits of gratitude, he decided to start a gratitude journal. Each night before bed, David would write down three things he was grateful for that day. At first, it was challenging to find things to be grateful for, but over time, it became easier. David noticed that his anxiety began to lessen, and he felt more at peace. By focusing on the positive aspects of his life, David was able to maintain mental clarity and reduce the impact of negative thoughts.

## 3. Setting Clear Boundaries: Protecting Your Mental Space

Boundaries are essential for maintaining mental clarity. Without clear boundaries, you may find yourself overwhelmed by the demands and expectations of others, leading to mental clutter. By setting and enforcing boundaries, you can protect your mental space and maintain clarity.

**Practical Advice:** Start by identifying areas in your life where you need to set boundaries. This could be at work, with family, or in your social life. For example, if you find that work emails or messages are intruding on your personal time, set a boundary by turning off notifications after a certain hour or establishing specific times for checking and responding to emails.

It's also important to communicate your boundaries clearly to others. Let people know when you're available and when you need uninterrupted time for yourself. Don't be afraid to say no to requests or commitments that don't align with your priorities or that could contribute to mental clutter.

**Story Example:** Lisa, a freelance writer, often found herself working late into the night because clients would contact her at all hours with urgent requests. This constant intrusion into her personal time left her feeling exhausted and mentally drained. Realizing she needed to protect her mental space, Lisa decided to set clear boundaries with her clients. She informed them of her working hours and let them know that she would not respond to emails or messages outside of those hours. By enforcing these boundaries, Lisa was able to reclaim her evenings for relaxation and self-care, which helped her maintain mental clarity and improve her overall well-being.

## 4. Regularly Evaluating and Adjusting Your Priorities

Mental clarity is closely tied to how well you manage your priorities. When your priorities are clear, it's easier to stay focused and avoid the mental clutter that comes from trying to do too much at once. Regularly evaluating and adjusting your priorities ensures that you're always focused on what truly matters, helping you maintain mental clarity over time.

**Practical Advice:** Take time each week to review your goals and priorities. Reflect on what you've accomplished and assess whether your current focus aligns with your long-term objectives. If you find that certain tasks or commitments are no longer serving you, don't hesitate to let them go or delegate them to someone else.

Consider using tools like to-do lists, planners, or digital apps to keep track of your priorities and tasks. Breaking down larger goals into smaller, actionable steps can help you stay organized and reduce mental clutter.

**Story Example:** Mark, a small business owner, found himself constantly juggling multiple projects and responsibilities. Despite his best efforts, he often felt overwhelmed and struggled to stay focused. After attending a time management workshop, Mark began regularly evaluating his priorities. He started using a planner to map out his weekly goals and break them down into manageable tasks. This practice helped him stay on track and maintain mental clarity, even during busy periods. By focusing on his most important priorities, Mark was able to reduce mental clutter and achieve greater success in his business.

## 5. Engaging in Regular Physical Activity

Physical activity is not only beneficial for your body but also for your mind. Exercise has been shown to reduce stress, improve mood, and enhance cognitive function, all of which contribute to maintaining mental clarity. Regular physical activity helps to clear your mind, boost your energy levels, and improve your overall mental well-being.

**Practical Advice:** Incorporate physical activity into your daily routine, even if it's just a short walk or a quick workout. Find an activity that you enjoy, whether it's running, yoga, swimming, or dancing, and make it a regular part of your life. Exercise not only helps to clear mental clutter but also provides an opportunity to disconnect from stressors and focus on yourself.

Consider combining physical activity with mindfulness practices, such as mindful walking or yoga, to enhance the benefits for your mental clarity. These activities allow you to be present in the moment, helping you clear your mind and maintain focus.

**Story Example:** Maria, a software developer, often found herself sitting for long hours in front of her computer, which led to mental fatigue and difficulty concentrating. Realizing the impact on her mental clarity, Maria decided to incorporate regular physical activity into her routine. She started taking a 30-minute walk each morning before work and practicing yoga in the evenings. These activities helped her clear her mind, reduce stress, and improve her focus at work. By making physical activity a priority, Maria was able to maintain mental clarity and enhance her overall well-being.

## 6. Limiting Information Overload: Being Selective About Your Inputs

In today's digital age, we're constantly bombarded with information from various sources—social media, news outlets, emails, and more. While staying informed is important, too much information can lead to mental clutter and overwhelm. Limiting information overload is key to maintaining mental clarity.

**Practical Advice:** Be selective about the information you consume. Identify the sources that provide you with valuable, relevant information and limit your exposure to unnecessary or distracting content. Consider setting specific times for checking the news or social media, rather than constantly scrolling throughout the day.

Another effective strategy is to practice digital minimalism—decluttering your digital space by unsubscribing from email lists, deleting unused apps, and organizing your files and folders. By reducing the amount of information you take in, you can free up mental space and maintain clarity.

**Story Example:** Alex, a student, found himself constantly distracted by social media and news updates, which affected his ability to focus on his studies. Realizing the impact of information overload on his mental clarity, Alex decided to implement a digital detox. He unfollowed unnecessary accounts on social media, limited his news consumption to once a day, and set specific times for checking his phone. These changes helped Alex reduce distractions and maintain mental clarity, allowing him to concentrate better on his studies and achieve his academic goals.

# Chapter 5: Decluttering Your Relationships— Building Stronger Connections

# Section 1: Recognizing Toxic Relationships—Identifying What's Holding You Back

Toxic relationships can be one of the most significant sources of emotional and mental clutter in our lives. They drain our energy, damage our self-esteem, and hold us back from reaching our full potential. Recognizing these toxic relationships is the first step toward creating healthier connections and decluttering your life. In this section, we'll explore how to identify toxic relationships, understand their impact, and take actionable steps to distance yourself from them.

## 1. Understanding the Impact of Toxic Relationships

Toxic relationships can take many forms, from friendships and romantic partnerships to family dynamics and professional connections. What makes a relationship toxic is its consistently harmful impact on your well-being. These relationships are characterized by negativity, manipulation, control, or emotional abuse. Over time, they can erode your mental health, self-worth, and happiness.

**Practical Advice:** Start by reflecting on how you feel after interacting with someone. If you frequently feel drained, anxious, or upset after spending time with a particular person, it's a strong indicator that the relationship may be toxic. Pay attention to patterns of behaviour—are your interactions consistently negative, or do they leave you feeling unsupported or belittled?

**Story Example:** Jessica, a 32-year-old graphic designer, had been friends with Emily since college. Over the years, she noticed that after spending time with Emily, she often felt emotionally exhausted and insecure. Emily would frequently criticize Jessica's choices, make sarcastic comments about her achievements, and dismiss her feelings when she tried to share something personal. Jessica initially brushed it off, thinking it was just Emily's way of being honest, but the negativity began to weigh heavily on her.

It wasn't until Jessica started feeling anxious before meeting Emily that she realized something was seriously wrong. She decided to step back and reflect on the friendship. She noticed that Emily rarely offered support or encouragement; instead, their interactions were often filled with subtle put-downs and passive-aggressive remarks. Recognizing the toxic nature of the relationship, Jessica knew she needed to distance herself for the sake of her mental health.

## 2. Signs of a Toxic Relationship: Red Flags to Watch For

Recognizing a toxic relationship isn't always straightforward, especially if you've been in it for a long time. However, there are specific red flags that can help you identify when a relationship is doing more harm than good. These signs include:

- **Constant Criticism or Judgment:** A toxic person often criticizes or judges you, making you feel inadequate or unworthy. This criticism may be disguised as "constructive feedback," but it consistently undermines your confidence and self-esteem.

- **Manipulation and Control:** Toxic individuals may try to control your actions, decisions, or emotions. They might use guilt, fear, or manipulation to get what they want, leaving you feeling powerless or trapped.

- **Lack of Support:** In healthy relationships, there is mutual support and encouragement. In a toxic relationship, however, you may find that the other person rarely, if ever, offers genuine support. Instead, they may downplay your achievements or dismiss your feelings.

- **Emotional Rollercoaster:** Toxic relationships are often characterized by extreme highs and lows. You may experience brief moments of happiness followed by long periods of conflict, tension, or sadness.

- **Blame and Guilt:** A toxic person may never take responsibility for their actions and instead blame you for any issues in the relationship. They might also make you feel guilty for setting boundaries or prioritizing your needs.

**Practical Advice:** Take some time to assess your relationships using these red flags as a guide. Write down specific examples of behaviours that have made you feel uncomfortable or hurt. This exercise can help you gain clarity about whether a relationship is toxic and whether it's worth addressing or walking away from.

**Story Example:** Tom, a 40-year-old accountant, was in a long-term relationship with his partner, Lisa. At first, their relationship seemed perfect—Lisa was charming, attentive, and loving. However, as time went on, Tom began to notice that Lisa would often criticize him, from his appearance to his career choices. Whenever Tom tried to discuss his feelings, Lisa would dismiss them, saying he was too sensitive or overreacting.

Tom also realized that Lisa was very controlling. She would get upset if he spent time with friends or pursued hobbies without her. She frequently used guilt to manipulate him into doing things her way, and when things didn't go according to her plan, she would blame Tom for the problems in their relationship.

Over time, Tom began to feel like he was walking on eggshells, constantly trying to avoid upsetting Lisa. He noticed that he was losing his sense of self and becoming increasingly anxious. After reflecting on their relationship and discussing it with a close friend, Tom recognized the toxic dynamics at play. He made the difficult decision to end the relationship and focus on rebuilding his self-worth and happiness.

## 3. Breaking Free: How to Distance Yourself from Toxicity

Once you've recognized a toxic relationship, the next step is to distance yourself from it. This process can be challenging, especially if the relationship is with someone close to you, like a family member, long-time friend, or partner. However, prioritizing your well-being is essential, and distancing yourself from toxic individuals is a necessary part of decluttering your life.

**Practical Advice:** The first step in distancing yourself from a toxic relationship is setting clear boundaries. Communicate your needs and expectations openly and assertively. For example, if someone is constantly negative or critical, let them know that you will no longer engage in conversations that make you feel bad about yourself. Be firm in enforcing these boundaries, even if it means limiting or cutting off contact with the person.

If the relationship is particularly harmful or abusive, consider seeking support from a therapist or counsellor. They can provide guidance on how to safely distance yourself and offer strategies for coping with the emotional aftermath.

Another important step is surrounding yourself with positive, supportive people. Building a network of friends, family members, or colleagues who uplift and encourage you can help fill the void left by distancing yourself from toxic individuals.

**Story Example:** Maria, a 29-year-old nurse, had a strained relationship with her mother, who was highly critical and emotionally manipulative. Growing up, Maria's mother would belittle her achievements, compare her to others, and guilt-trip her into doing things she didn't want to do. As an adult, Maria found herself feeling anxious and depressed after every interaction with her mother.

Maria decided it was time to set boundaries. She had a candid conversation with her mother, explaining how her behaviour was affecting her and setting limits on their interactions. For example, Maria limited phone calls to once a week and decided not to engage in conversations that involved criticism or manipulation. When her mother tried to push those boundaries, Maria remained firm, calmly ending the conversation when necessary.

While it was difficult at first, Maria found that setting boundaries helped her regain control over her emotional well-being. She also leaned on her friends and her partner for support, which helped her stay strong during the challenging transition. Over time, Maria's mental health improved, and she felt more empowered and at peace.

## 4. The Role of Self-Reflection and Forgiveness

Self-reflection is a crucial part of recognizing and addressing toxic relationships. It allows you to understand why you may have tolerated toxic behaviour in the past and what steps you can take to prevent similar situations in the future. Forgiveness, both for yourself and others, can also play a role in the healing process, helping you move forward without carrying the weight of resentment or guilt.

**Practical Advice:** Take time to reflect on your past relationships and consider what you've learned from them. Ask yourself why you stayed in toxic situations—was it fear of loneliness, a desire for approval, or something else? Understanding your motivations can help you make healthier choices moving forward.

Forgiveness doesn't mean excusing harmful behaviour or allowing it to continue. Instead, it's about letting go of the anger or hurt that can keep you tied to the past. Forgive yourself for any mistakes you may have made, and focus on building healthier relationships in the future.

**Story Example:** Kevin, a 45-year-old teacher, struggled with feelings of resentment toward his brother, who had always been manipulative and self-centered. Despite this, Kevin found it hard to distance himself, feeling obligated to maintain a close relationship because they were family.

After attending a personal development workshop, Kevin began to reflect on why he felt compelled to stay close to his brother, despite the toxicity. He realized that much of it stemmed from a sense of duty and guilt, coupled with a desire for his brother's approval. With this insight, Kevin decided to set boundaries, limiting their interactions to family gatherings and focusing on building relationships with other supportive family members.

Kevin also worked on forgiving his brother—not for the sake of reconciliation, but to free himself from the burden of anger and resentment. This process allowed Kevin to move forward with a lighter heart and more clarity about the kind of relationships he wanted in his life.

# Section 2: Nurturing Positive Relationships—Fostering Meaningful Connections

While recognizing and distancing yourself from toxic relationships is essential, cultivating and nurturing positive relationships is just as crucial for your well-being and personal growth. Positive relationships are the ones that uplift you, provide mutual support, and help you thrive. In this section, we'll explore practical strategies for fostering meaningful connections in your life, emphasizing the importance of communication, trust, respect, and the value of quality over quantity in your social circle.

## 1. The Power of Positive Relationships on Mental and Emotional Well-being

Positive relationships are a cornerstone of a happy and fulfilling life. Research has shown that strong, supportive connections with others contribute significantly to mental and emotional well-being. These relationships provide a sense of belonging, reduce stress, and increase overall life satisfaction. In contrast to toxic relationships, which drain your energy and leave you feeling depleted, positive relationships replenish your emotional reserves and help you navigate life's challenges with resilience and optimism.

**Practical Advice:** Take an inventory of the relationships in your life. Identify those that bring you joy, support, and a sense of belonging. Make a conscious effort to invest more time and energy into these connections. Whether it's scheduling regular catch-ups with a close friend or making time for family, prioritizing these relationships will enhance your mental and emotional well-being.

**Story Example:** Sarah, a 28-year-old marketing professional, had always been close to her cousin, Amy. Despite living in different cities, they made an effort to stay connected through regular phone calls and visits. Sarah realized that her relationship with Amy was one of the most positive and supportive in her life. Amy was always there to listen, offer advice, and celebrate Sarah's successes. During a particularly stressful period at work, Sarah found that talking to Amy helped her stay grounded and optimistic. Recognizing the value of this connection, Sarah decided to prioritize their relationship even more, ensuring they stayed close despite the distance.

## 2. How to Strengthen Your Bonds: Communication, Trust, and Mutual Respect

The foundation of any positive relationship is strong communication, trust, and mutual respect. These elements are essential for creating and maintaining meaningful connections that stand the test of time.

**Communication:** Open and honest communication is the key to understanding and being understood in any relationship. It involves not only expressing your thoughts and feelings clearly but also listening actively to the other person. Effective communication helps prevent misunderstandings, resolve conflicts, and deepen your connection.

**Practical Advice:** Practice active listening in your conversations. This means giving your full attention to the other person, acknowledging their feelings, and responding thoughtfully. Avoid interrupting or jumping to conclusions. Instead, ask questions to clarify their point of view and express empathy. This approach fosters a deeper understanding and strengthens your bond.

**Story Example:** John and Emily had been married for five years, and like many couples, they experienced their share of conflicts. John often felt that Emily didn't understand his perspective, leading to arguments that left both of them frustrated. After attending a couples' workshop on communication, John realized that he hadn't been truly listening to Emily. He would often interrupt her or assume he knew what she was going to say. By practicing active listening—really hearing Emily out without interruption and reflecting on her feelings—John noticed a significant improvement in their relationship. Their conversations became more meaningful, and they were able to resolve conflicts more effectively, bringing them closer together.

**Trust:** Trust is the bedrock of any strong relationship. It involves believing in the other person's integrity, reliability, and good intentions. Trust allows you to feel secure and supported, knowing that the other person has your best interests at heart. Building trust takes time, but once established, it can create a deep sense of connection and loyalty.

**Practical Advice:** Build trust in your relationships by being consistent, reliable, and honest. Follow through on your commitments, communicate openly, and show that you value the other person's trust in you. If trust has been broken, acknowledge the mistake, take responsibility, and work to rebuild it through consistent actions and transparent communication.

**Story Example:** Laura and her best friend, Rachel, had known each other since childhood. Over the years, they had built a strong foundation of trust, sharing their deepest secrets and supporting each other through life's ups and downs. However, when Laura accidentally let slip something Rachel had confided in her, Rachel felt betrayed. Laura realized the gravity of her mistake and took immediate action to repair the trust. She apologized sincerely, explained what had happened, and made a commitment to be more careful in the future. Laura also made an effort to show Rachel how much she valued their friendship by being more attentive and reliable. Over time, Rachel forgave Laura, and their trust was restored, ultimately strengthening their bond.

**Mutual Respect:** Respect is the recognition and appreciation of each other's differences, boundaries, and individuality. In positive relationships, respect is a two-way street—both parties acknowledge each other's value and treat each other with kindness and consideration. Respecting someone means honouring their opinions, feelings, and choices, even if they differ from your own.

**Practical Advice:** Cultivate mutual respect in your relationships by practicing empathy and being mindful of the other person's boundaries. Avoid making assumptions about their thoughts or feelings, and instead, ask for their perspective. Show appreciation for their unique qualities and be willing to compromise when necessary. Respect is shown not only through words but also through actions—small gestures of kindness and consideration go a long way in building a strong, respectful relationship.

**Story Example:** Mark, a 35-year-old teacher, had a close friendship with his colleague, Tom. Despite their different teaching styles and approaches to problem-solving, they respected each other's methods and valued what the other brought to the table. When they had disagreements, they approached them with a willingness to listen and understand each other's point of view. This mutual respect allowed them to collaborate effectively and maintain a strong friendship, even in the face of challenges. Their respect for each other's individuality and professional expertise made their working relationship one of the most positive and rewarding aspects of their careers.

## 3. Prioritizing Quality over Quantity in Your Social Circle

In today's social media-driven world, it's easy to fall into the trap of equating the number of connections with the strength of your social network. However, research shows that the quality of your relationships is far more important than the quantity. A few deep, meaningful connections can provide more emotional support and satisfaction than a large number of superficial ones.

**Practical Advice:** Focus on cultivating a small circle of close, trusted relationships rather than trying to maintain a vast network of acquaintances. Invest your time and energy in the relationships that matter most—those that bring you joy, support, and a sense of belonging. It's better to have a few friends who truly understand and care about you than to spread yourself thin across numerous shallow connections.

**Story Example:** After moving to a new city, Emily felt pressured to expand her social circle quickly. She attended numerous social events, trying to make as many new friends as possible. However, she soon realized that these connections were mostly surface-level and left her feeling unfulfilled. Emily decided to take a different approach, focusing on deepening her relationships with a few people she genuinely connected with. She started spending more time with her neighbour, Sarah, and a colleague from work, both of whom shared her interests and values. These relationships grew stronger over time, providing Emily with the meaningful connections she had been searching for.

# Section 3: Setting Boundaries and Managing Expectations—Creating Healthy Relationship Dynamics

Establishing healthy relationship dynamics is essential for fostering positive and supportive connections. A critical aspect of this process involves setting clear boundaries and managing expectations, which can help you navigate interactions with others while preserving your well-being. In this section, we will explore the importance of boundaries and expectations, practical strategies for setting and maintaining them, and how doing so can lead to healthier, more fulfilling relationships.

## 1. The Importance of Boundaries in Relationships

Boundaries are the invisible lines that define your personal limits—what you are comfortable with and what you are not. They are essential in all types of relationships, whether with family, friends, or colleagues. Boundaries help you protect your emotional, mental, and physical well-being by ensuring that your needs are met and that you are treated with respect. Without clear boundaries, relationships can become strained, leading to feelings of resentment, burnout, and even conflict.

**Practical Advice:** Start by identifying your personal boundaries. Consider what makes you feel uncomfortable or drained in your relationships, and what behaviors or situations you want to avoid. Once you've identified these boundaries, communicate them clearly and assertively to the people in your life. Remember, setting boundaries is not about being rigid or unkind—it's about creating a space where you can thrive.

**Story Example:** Maria, a 34-year-old nurse, was always the go-to person for her friends and family. She loved helping others, but over time, she started to feel overwhelmed by the constant demands on her time and energy. Maria realized that she was often saying "yes" to requests even when she wanted to say "no." This left her feeling exhausted and resentful. After attending a workshop on boundaries, Maria decided to set clearer limits in her relationships. She learned to say "no" when she needed to, without feeling guilty. She also started communicating her boundaries more effectively, letting her loved ones know that while she valued them, she also needed time for herself. As a result, Maria felt more balanced and empowered in her relationships, and her connections with others became more respectful and supportive.

## 2. Strategies for Setting and Communicating Boundaries

Setting boundaries is one thing, but communicating them effectively is another challenge. Clear and assertive communication is key to ensuring that your boundaries are understood and respected. Here are some practical strategies to help you set and communicate boundaries in a way that strengthens your relationships rather than creating conflict.

**Be Clear and Specific:** When setting boundaries, it's important to be clear and specific about what you need. Vague or ambiguous boundaries can lead to misunderstandings and frustration. For example, instead of saying, "I need some space," you could say, "I need an hour of alone time each evening to recharge."

**Practical Advice:** Practice using "I" statements when communicating your boundaries. This helps you express your needs without sounding accusatory or confrontational. For example, "I need time to focus on my work, so I won't be able to take on extra tasks right now," is more effective than, "You're always giving me too much work."

**Story Example:** Jason, a 29-year-old software developer, was constantly bombarded with work-related messages from his boss, even after hours. This was affecting his work-life balance and causing him stress. Jason decided to set a boundary around his availability outside of work hours. He approached his boss and explained, "I've noticed that responding to work messages after hours is impacting my ability to recharge. I need to focus on my personal time in the evenings, so unless it's an emergency, I won't be responding to messages after 7 PM." Jason's boss respected his boundary, and Jason felt more in control of his time, which improved his overall well-being.

**Be Consistent:** Once you've set a boundary, it's crucial to be consistent in enforcing it. Inconsistency can send mixed signals to others, leading them to believe that your boundaries are negotiable. Consistency reinforces your commitment to your own well-being and helps others understand that your boundaries are non-negotiable.

**Practical Advice:** If someone crosses your boundary, address it immediately and reaffirm your limits. For example, if a friend continues to drop by unannounced despite your request for advance notice, gently remind them of your boundary: "I appreciate your visits, but I need a heads-up before you come over. Please call or text me first."

**Story Example:** Lily, a 40-year-old teacher, had a close friend, Anna, who often borrowed money from her but rarely paid it back. Lily felt uncomfortable with this dynamic but didn't want to strain their friendship. After reflecting on her boundaries, Lily decided to set a limit on lending money. The next time Anna asked to borrow money, Lily politely declined, explaining, "I've realized that lending money affects our friendship in ways I'm not comfortable with, so I'm no longer able to lend money to friends." Although Anna was initially upset, she respected Lily's boundary, and their friendship improved as a result.

## 3. Managing Expectations in Relationships

Expectations play a significant role in how we perceive and interact with others. When expectations are realistic and clearly communicated, they can enhance relationships by aligning intentions and actions. However, unmet or unspoken expectations can lead to disappointment, frustration, and conflict. Managing expectations involves understanding your own needs and desires, as well as those of others, and ensuring that they are realistic and mutually agreed upon.

**Practical Advice:** Take time to reflect on the expectations you have in your relationships. Are they realistic? Have you communicated them clearly? Are you holding others to standards that they may not be aware of? Similarly, consider the expectations others may have of you. Are they reasonable, and do they align with your own values and boundaries?

**Story Example:** Sarah and her husband, Tom, had been married for several years. Over time, Sarah noticed that she was growing frustrated with Tom for not helping more around the house. She had expected that he would automatically take on more responsibilities without her having to ask. However, she realized that this expectation was unspoken and that Tom might not even be aware of it. Sarah decided to have an open conversation with Tom about her expectations. She explained how she felt and asked for his help with specific tasks. Tom was receptive and willing to contribute more once he understood what Sarah needed. By managing her expectations and communicating them clearly, Sarah was able to create a more balanced and supportive dynamic in their marriage.

**Reevaluating Expectations:** As relationships evolve, so do expectations. What may have been reasonable at one stage of your relationship may no longer be appropriate or realistic later on. Regularly reevaluating your expectations helps ensure that they remain aligned with the current state of the relationship and that both parties are on the same page.

**Practical Advice:** Schedule regular check-ins with your loved ones to discuss how your relationship is evolving and whether any adjustments to your expectations are needed. This proactive approach helps prevent misunderstandings and ensures that your relationship continues to grow in a healthy direction.

**Story Example:** After the birth of their first child, Emma and James found that their expectations of each other as partners had shifted. Emma expected James to take on more household responsibilities, while James assumed that Emma would handle most of the childcare. This led to tension and resentment on both sides. Realizing that their expectations were no longer aligned, they decided to sit down and discuss their new roles and responsibilities. By openly communicating and adjusting their expectations, Emma and James were able to find a balance that worked for both of them, strengthening their partnership in the process.

**Balancing Expectations and Boundaries:** While setting boundaries is essential, it's equally important to balance them with realistic expectations. Sometimes, we may need to adjust our boundaries to meet the expectations of a relationship, and vice versa. The key is to find a balance that respects both your needs and those of the other person.

**Practical Advice:** When balancing boundaries and expectations, consider the needs of the relationship as a whole. Are there areas where you can be more flexible without compromising your well-being? Conversely, are there expectations that need to be adjusted to better align with your boundaries? Open and honest communication is crucial in finding this balance.

**Story Example:** Rachel, a 32-year-old graphic designer, had a close-knit group of friends who often relied on her for help with their creative projects. While Rachel loved supporting her friends, she found that constantly saying "yes" was cutting into her personal time and affecting her work-life balance. Rachel decided to set a boundary around the amount of time she could dedicate to helping others. She communicated this to her friends, explaining that while she valued their friendship, she needed to prioritize her own work and well-being. At the same time, Rachel adjusted her expectations of herself, recognizing that it was okay to say "no" sometimes. By balancing her boundaries with her expectations, Rachel was able to maintain her friendships while also taking care of herself.

# Chapter 6: Decluttering Your Health—Creating Space for Wellness

# Section 1: The Connection Between Clutter and Health—Understanding the Impact

Clutter is often dismissed as a minor annoyance, but its effects on health are far from trivial. The impact of clutter extends beyond the physical space it occupies; it infiltrates mental and emotional well-being, disrupts sleep, and even undermines physical health. Understanding the connection between clutter and health is crucial for making informed decisions about how to create a space that nurtures well-being. In this section, we'll explore how clutter affects physical health, mental and emotional well-being, and sleep, offering practical advice and real-world examples to illustrate the profound effects of a cluttered environment on overall health.

## Physical Health and Clutter

Clutter can have a significant impact on physical health in ways that might not be immediately apparent. When a space is cluttered, it becomes harder to maintain cleanliness, which can lead to an accumulation of dust, mold, and allergens. These environmental hazards can trigger respiratory issues such as allergies and asthma. Additionally, cluttered spaces increase the risk of accidents, with items strewn about that can easily be tripped over or cause injury.

**Practical Advice:** Start by decluttering areas that tend to accumulate the most dust and allergens, such as bedrooms, living rooms, and storage spaces. Regularly clean these areas to prevent the buildup of harmful particles. For those with allergies or asthma, it's essential to use a high-efficiency particulate air (HEPA) filter in your vacuum cleaner and air purifier to remove allergens from the air.

**Story Example:** Take the case of Linda, a 42-year-old mother of two who had struggled with asthma for years. Her home was filled with items she didn't need—old magazines, unused furniture, and toys her children had outgrown. Over time, the clutter made it difficult for her to clean thoroughly, leading to an increase in dust and allergens. Linda's asthma symptoms worsened, and she found herself using her inhaler more frequently. After attending a seminar on the health impacts of clutter, Linda decided to take action. She began by decluttering her home, room by room. She donated or discarded items that were no longer useful, deep-cleaned each space, and invested in an air purifier. Within weeks, Linda noticed a significant improvement in her asthma symptoms. She was able to reduce her reliance on medication, and her overall quality of life improved as her home became a healthier environment.

## Mental and Emotional Health

Clutter can have a profound effect on mental and emotional health. A cluttered environment often leads to feelings of overwhelm, anxiety, and stress. This is because clutter constantly sends signals to the brain that work is never done, leading to a perpetual state of tension. Moreover, the visual chaos of clutter can make it difficult to concentrate, reducing productivity and increasing frustration.

**Practical Advice:** To address mental and emotional clutter, start by creating a designated space for relaxation, free of distractions. This could be a corner of your living room, a spot in your bedroom, or even a small area on your balcony. Keep this space free of unnecessary items, and make it a habit to spend a few minutes there each day, practicing deep breathing or mindfulness exercises. This dedicated clutter-free zone can serve as a mental retreat, helping to alleviate stress and promote relaxation.

**Story Example:** Michael, a 35-year-old software developer, found himself increasingly anxious and unable to focus on his work. His apartment was cluttered with unfinished projects, paperwork, and personal items that he had no place for. The constant visual reminder of tasks left undone weighed heavily on his mind, leading to feelings of inadequacy and stress. Realizing that his environment was contributing to his mental clutter, Michael decided to make a change. He started by clearing out his workspace, organizing his files, and getting rid of items that no longer served a purpose. He also created a "mindfulness corner" in his living room, where he could sit and meditate or simply enjoy a moment of calm. As his physical space became more organized, Michael noticed a significant reduction in his anxiety levels. He was able to focus better at work, and his overall mental clarity improved. The act of decluttering had a transformative effect on his mental and emotional well-being.

## The Role of Sleep in Health

A cluttered environment can also disrupt sleep, which is a cornerstone of good health. The bedroom should be a sanctuary for rest, but when it's filled with clutter, it can become a source of stress rather than relaxation. Clutter in the bedroom can create a sense of chaos, making it difficult for the mind to unwind. Additionally, digital clutter—such as keeping electronic devices in the bedroom—can interfere with sleep patterns by exposing you to blue light, which suppresses the production of melatonin, a hormone that regulates sleep.

**Practical Advice:** To improve sleep quality, start by decluttering your bedroom. Remove unnecessary items from your bedside tables, floor, and surfaces. Keep only those things that contribute to a peaceful and restful environment, such as a lamp, a book, or a small plant. Additionally, consider creating a "digital sunset" routine, where you turn off all electronic devices at least an hour before bed. This will help reduce the impact of blue light and allow your mind to transition into sleep mode more effectively.

**Story Example:** Emma, a 28-year-old graphic designer, struggled with insomnia for months. Her bedroom was cluttered with clothes, gadgets, and work materials, which made it difficult for her to relax and fall asleep. She often found herself scrolling through her phone late at night, further disrupting her sleep patterns. Frustrated with her lack of rest, Emma decided to take action. She began by decluttering her bedroom, removing items that didn't contribute to a restful environment. She also implemented a digital sunset routine, turning off her phone and other devices an hour before bed. Within a few weeks, Emma noticed a significant improvement in her sleep quality. She was falling asleep faster and waking up feeling more refreshed. By decluttering her bedroom and reducing digital distractions, Emma was able to create a sleep-friendly environment that supported her health.

## The Cumulative Impact of Clutter on Health

While clutter's impact on physical, mental, and emotional health is significant in isolation, the cumulative effect of clutter across these areas can be even more profound. When clutter affects multiple aspects of your life, it can create a cycle of stress and overwhelm that's difficult to break. For example, a cluttered home can lead to poor physical health, which in turn exacerbates mental and emotional stress. This stress can then lead to poor sleep, which further impacts physical health, creating a vicious cycle.

**Practical Advice:** Breaking the cycle of clutter requires a holistic approach. Start by identifying the areas of your life where clutter has the most significant impact—whether it's your physical space, mental clarity, or sleep quality. Focus on decluttering one area at a time, making small, manageable changes that you can sustain over the long term. For example, if clutter is affecting your physical health, start by decluttering and deep cleaning one room in your home. If mental clutter is a concern, consider incorporating mindfulness practices into your daily routine. The key is to approach decluttering as an ongoing process rather than a one-time event.

**Story Example:** John, a 50-year-old accountant, had been struggling with high blood pressure and stress for years. His home was cluttered with decades of accumulated belongings, and the chaos made it difficult for him to relax or focus. His stress levels were high, which contributed to his health issues, including poor sleep and weight gain. Recognizing that his environment was a major contributor to his health problems, John decided to make a change. He started by decluttering his kitchen, clearing out old appliances and organizing his pantry to make it easier to prepare healthy meals. Next, he focused on his bedroom, creating a peaceful space free of distractions. Finally, John implemented a regular exercise routine to help manage his stress. Over time, John noticed significant improvements in his health—his blood pressure lowered, his stress levels decreased, and he began to sleep better. By addressing the clutter in his life, John was able to break the cycle of stress and improve his overall well-being.

# Section 2: Decluttering Your Diet and Exercise Routine—Simplifying Wellness

When it comes to health, we often focus on complicated diets and intense exercise regimens, believing that more is better. However, health and wellness don't have to be complex or overwhelming. In fact, simplifying your diet and exercise routine can make it easier to sustain long-term habits that support your physical and mental well-being. This section explores practical strategies for decluttering your approach to food and fitness, offering real-world advice and personal stories to make the process more relatable and achievable.

## Simplifying Your Diet: Focus on Nutrient-Dense, Whole Foods

In today's world, the sheer volume of dietary advice can be paralyzing. One diet suggests low carbs, another promotes plant-based eating, while a third encourages intermittent fasting. This abundance of options often leads to confusion, frustration, and unhealthy eating habits. Simplifying your diet by focusing on nutrient-dense, whole foods can alleviate much of this confusion and help you make more intentional, health-promoting choices.

**Practical Advice:**

1. **Choose Whole, Unprocessed Foods:** Rather than obsessing over specific diets, focus on whole, unprocessed foods. These are foods in their most natural state—fruits, vegetables, whole grains, lean proteins, and healthy fats. By prioritizing these options, you avoid the hidden sugars, unhealthy fats, and artificial ingredients that can contribute to poor health. The simplicity of a whole-foods-based diet also reduces the mental clutter that comes from overanalysing every meal choice.

2. **Limit Variety for Simplicity:** While variety is often considered the spice of life, too much variety in your diet can lead to decision fatigue. You don't need to eat a different dish every day of the week. Focus on a few simple, nutritious meals that you enjoy and rotate them throughout the week. This minimizes the mental effort required for meal planning and allows you to streamline grocery shopping and cooking.

3. **Batch Cooking and Meal Prep:** One way to declutter your diet is by batch cooking and meal prepping. Spend one or two days a week preparing larger portions of meals, which you can then store and eat throughout the week. This not only reduces the time spent in the kitchen each day but also makes it easier to stick to healthy choices when you're busy.

**Story Example:**

Sarah, a 30-year-old marketing executive, constantly found herself overwhelmed by the choices and complexities of healthy eating. After trying countless diets that left her feeling drained and guilty, she realized that she needed a simpler approach. She began focusing on whole foods and eliminated processed snacks and take-out from her diet. Instead of trying to cook a new recipe every night, she started batch-cooking on Sundays. Sarah found that by simplifying her approach, she was able to enjoy her meals without stressing over calories or ingredients. As a result, she lost weight, gained energy, and found herself actually enjoying the process of preparing and eating healthy food.

## Streamlining Your Exercise Routine: Quality Over Quantity

Exercise is essential for maintaining physical health, but the pressure to commit to long, intense workouts often leads to burnout or avoidance. Many people struggle to find time to exercise regularly, and when they do, they often follow plans that are too complicated or demanding. Streamlining your exercise routine by focusing on quality over quantity can make fitness more manageable, sustainable, and enjoyable.

**Practical Advice:**

1. **Choose Activities You Enjoy:** One of the simplest ways to declutter your exercise routine is by focusing on activities that you genuinely enjoy. Exercise doesn't have to mean hours at the gym or complicated workout programs. If you love walking, dancing, or swimming, incorporate those activities into your routine. By choosing exercises that feel enjoyable rather than like a chore, you'll be more motivated to stick with them in the long term.

2. **Prioritize Functional Movement:** Functional movement refers to exercises that mimic everyday activities and improve your ability to perform daily tasks. Squats, lunges, push-ups, and planks are examples of exercises that target multiple muscle groups at once, making your workout more efficient. These movements don't require expensive gym equipment or complicated routines, and they can be done anywhere, whether at home or in the park.

3. **Shorten Workout Times:** High-intensity interval training (HIIT) is a great way to streamline your fitness routine. HIIT involves short bursts of intense exercise followed by brief periods of rest, and it has been proven to be highly effective in improving cardiovascular health, strength, and endurance. These workouts can be completed in as little as 20-30 minutes, making them ideal for people with busy schedules. Shorter, high-quality workouts are more sustainable and less likely to lead to burnout.

**Story Example:**

Mike, a 40-year-old father of two, struggled to fit regular exercise into his packed schedule. He felt guilty for not spending enough time at the gym and often gave up on working out altogether. After reading about HIIT and functional movement, Mike realized that he didn't need to dedicate hours to exercise in order to stay healthy. He started doing 20-minute HIIT sessions three times a week in his living room and incorporated bodyweight exercises like push-ups and squats into his daily routine. This simplified approach allowed Mike to stay active without sacrificing time with his family. Over time, he noticed improvements in his strength, energy levels, and overall fitness, all while spending less time exercising.

## The Power of Mindful Eating and Movement

Mindfulness is a powerful tool for decluttering both your diet and exercise routine. By practicing mindfulness, you can develop a more intentional relationship with food and exercise, leading to healthier choices and a more balanced approach to wellness. Mindfulness helps you tune into your body's natural signals, so you can eat and move in ways that feel nourishing rather than stressful or forced.

**Practical Advice:**

1. **Mindful Eating:**

   One of the main causes of poor eating habits is mindless consumption—eating while distracted, bored, or stressed. To declutter your diet, practice mindful eating. This means paying attention to your food—its taste, texture, and how it makes you feel. Slow down during meals, savor each bite, and stop eating when you feel satisfied, rather than full. Mindful eating helps you build a healthier relationship with food and prevents overeating.

2. **Mindful Movement:**

   Just as mindfulness can improve your relationship with food, it can also enhance your approach to exercise. Pay attention to how your body feels during exercise and focus on the sensations of movement. This can help you become more attuned to your body's needs and reduce the tendency to overtrain or push yourself too hard. Mindful movement encourages a more sustainable, enjoyable exercise routine.

**Story Example:**

Lisa, a 29-year-old teacher, had always struggled with emotional eating. After stressful days at work, she would often binge on junk food, only to feel guilty afterward. When she discovered mindful eating, Lisa decided to give it a try. She started eating her meals without distractions—no phone, no TV—and focused on the taste and texture of each bite. She noticed that she felt fuller faster and was less likely to overeat. At the same time, she began practicing yoga, paying close attention to her body's movements and sensations during each session. This mindful approach transformed Lisa's relationship with both food and exercise, helping her feel more balanced, in control, and healthier overall.

## Creating a Balanced, Sustainable Approach to Wellness

A decluttered diet and exercise routine isn't about deprivation or rigid rules—it's about finding balance and sustainability. Simplifying these areas of your life allows you to focus on what truly matters: nourishing your body and staying active in ways that feel natural and enjoyable.

**Practical Advice:**

1. **Set Realistic Goals:**

One of the biggest mistakes people make when trying to improve their health is setting overly ambitious goals that lead to frustration and burnout. To declutter your wellness routine, set small, realistic goals that you can achieve without overwhelming yourself. For example, instead of aiming to lose 10 pounds in a month, focus on eating more whole foods and incorporating daily movement. Small, incremental changes are more sustainable and lead to lasting results.

2. **Practice Self-Compassion:**

When decluttering your diet and exercise routine, it's important to be kind to yourself. Wellness is a journey, not a destination, and it's okay to have setbacks. Practicing self-compassion will help you stay motivated and prevent the cycle of guilt and shame that often accompanies unhealthy habits. Instead of focusing on perfection, aim for progress and celebrate the small wins along the way.

**Story Example:**

David, a 45-year-old accountant, had spent years yo-yo dieting and going through phases of intense exercise followed by complete inactivity. Tired of the constant cycle, he decided to simplify his approach to wellness. David set small, realistic goals, such as eating one healthy meal per day and going for a 30-minute walk three times a week. He also learned to be kinder to himself when he slipped up, focusing on progress rather than perfection. This mindset shift allowed David to build healthy habits that were sustainable long-term, and over time, he lost weight, improved his fitness, and felt more in control of his health than ever before.

# Section 3: Creating a Health-Focused Environment—Supporting Your Wellness Journey

The environment you live in has a profound impact on your health and well-being. Creating a health-focused environment is not just about making your space look good; it's about setting up your surroundings in a way that supports your wellness journey. Whether it's your home, workplace, or even your social environment, aligning these spaces with your health goals can make a significant difference in your ability to sustain a healthy lifestyle. In this section, we'll explore practical strategies to help you create an environment that nurtures your physical, mental, and emotional health.

## Decluttering Your Physical Space for Health

A cluttered home can lead to a cluttered mind, and both can negatively impact your health. By creating a physical environment that promotes wellness, you can reduce stress, improve your mood, and make it easier to stick to healthy habits.

**Practical Advice:**

1. **Create a Clean, Organized Kitchen:**

   The kitchen is the heart of the home, and it's also where your health journey begins. A cluttered kitchen can lead to poor food choices, as it's harder to find and prepare healthy meals. Start by decluttering your kitchen—clear out old, expired food, and remove unhealthy snacks from easy-to-reach places. Organize your pantry and fridge so that healthy options are front and center. Consider setting up designated areas for meal prep, cooking, and clean-up to streamline your time in the kitchen and make healthy eating more convenient.

2. **Designate Wellness Zones:**

   Your home should have spaces that are dedicated to specific wellness activities. For example, create a quiet, comfortable area for meditation or yoga, free from distractions and clutter. Designate another space for exercise, whether it's a corner of your living room for at-home workouts or a garage gym. Having these wellness zones makes it easier to incorporate healthy activities into your daily routine and reinforces the importance of these practices in your life.

### 3.  **Use Natural Elements to Boost Mood:**

Incorporating natural elements into your living space can have a calming effect and promote a sense of well-being. Consider adding plants to your home, which can improve air quality and create a more serene atmosphere. Use natural light as much as possible by opening curtains or blinds during the day. You can also incorporate natural materials, such as wood or stone, in your décor to create a more grounding environment.

**Story Example:**

Emma, a 35-year-old nurse, used to come home after long shifts to a cluttered, chaotic apartment. She found that the state of her home was contributing to her stress levels and making it difficult to unwind. After realizing the impact her environment was having on her health, Emma decided to make some changes. She decluttered her kitchen and organized her pantry, making it easier to prepare healthy meals. She also created a small meditation corner in her bedroom, complete with a comfortable cushion and soothing décor. Emma added a few houseplants and rearranged her furniture to maximize natural light. These changes transformed her apartment into a sanctuary that supported her wellness goals, and she noticed a significant improvement in her stress levels and overall well-being.

## Optimizing Your Workspace for Health and Productivity

For many people, the workplace is where they spend a significant portion of their day. Whether you work from home or in an office, the environment in which you work can have a direct impact on your health, productivity, and overall well-being. Optimizing your workspace to support your wellness goals can help you stay focused, energized, and healthy throughout the workday.

**Practical Advice:**

1. **Ergonomic Setup:**

   An ergonomic workspace setup is essential for preventing physical strain and promoting comfort during long hours of work. Invest in a chair that supports your back, and adjust your desk and monitor height to reduce strain on your neck and shoulders. Ensure that your keyboard and mouse are positioned to keep your wrists in a neutral position. This setup can help prevent common issues such as back pain, eye strain, and repetitive strain injuries.

2. **Incorporate Movement Breaks:**

Sitting for extended periods can be detrimental to your health. To counteract the negative effects of prolonged sitting, incorporate regular movement breaks into your workday. Set a timer to remind yourself to stand up, stretch, and move around every hour. Consider using a standing desk or alternating between sitting and standing throughout the day. These small adjustments can boost circulation, reduce fatigue, and improve focus.

3. **Minimize Distractions:**

A cluttered and distracting workspace can hinder productivity and increase stress. Keep your desk clean and organized, with only essential items within reach. Use noise-cancelling headphones or white noise to block out distractions if you work in a noisy environment. If you work from home, create a designated workspace that is separate from areas where you relax or socialize. This separation helps to create boundaries between work and personal life, reducing stress and improving focus.

**Story Example:**

Tom, a 42-year-old graphic designer, used to work from a cluttered desk in the corner of his living room. He often found himself distracted by the noise and activity around him, and his back pain from sitting in an uncomfortable chair was becoming unbearable. Realizing that his workspace was affecting his health and productivity, Tom decided to optimize his environment. He invested in an ergonomic chair and a standing desk converter, which allowed him to alternate between sitting and standing throughout the day. He also set up a separate workspace in a quiet room, free from distractions. By making these changes, Tom was able to work more efficiently, reduce his back pain, and maintain better focus throughout the day.

**Fostering a Health-Focused Social Environment**

Your social environment plays a crucial role in supporting or hindering your wellness journey. The people you surround yourself with can either encourage healthy habits or reinforce unhealthy ones. By fostering a health-focused social environment, you can build a network of support that helps you stay on track with your wellness goals.

**Practical Advice:**

1. **Surround Yourself with Supportive People:**

   The people you spend time with can have a significant impact on your health and well-being. Surround yourself with friends, family, and colleagues who support your wellness goals and encourage you to make healthy choices. This might mean spending less time with individuals who have habits that conflict with your goals, such as overeating, smoking, or leading a sedentary lifestyle. Instead, seek out social circles that prioritize activities like group workouts, healthy eating, or outdoor adventures.

2. **Engage in Health-Focused Social Activities:**

   Instead of meeting friends for drinks or meals, consider organizing health-focused social activities. This could include going for a hike, taking a yoga class together, or even cooking a healthy meal as a group. These activities not only support your health goals but also reinforce the importance of wellness within your social circle. By making health a shared value, you create an environment that encourages everyone to stay active and make healthy choices.

## 3. **Set Boundaries for Social Engagements:**

Social pressures can often lead to unhealthy behaviour, such as overeating at parties or skipping workouts to spend time with friends. To maintain a health-focused environment, it's important to set boundaries for social engagements. This might mean limiting your attendance at events where you're likely to be tempted by unhealthy choices, or it could involve setting a rule for yourself to always eat a healthy meal before attending a party. By setting these boundaries, you can enjoy social interactions without compromising your wellness journey.

**Story Example:**

Laura, a 28-year-old teacher, found that her social life was making it difficult to stick to her health goals. She often felt pressured to indulge in unhealthy foods and drinks when she was out with friends, and she struggled to find time for exercise. After reflecting on the impact her social environment was having on her health, Laura decided to make some changes. She started inviting her friends to join her for healthy activities, like weekend hikes and fitness classes, instead of going out to eat or drink. Laura also began setting boundaries around her social engagements, such as politely declining invitations to events that didn't align with her health goals. Over time, Laura noticed that her friends became more supportive of her wellness journey, and she felt more in control of her health while still enjoying a fulfilling social life.

## Creating a Wellness-Centric Digital Environment

In the digital age, the environment we create online is just as important as our physical and social surroundings. The content you consume and the interactions you engage in online can influence your mental and emotional well-being. By curating a wellness-centric digital environment, you can reduce stress, improve focus, and stay aligned with your health goals.

**Practical Advice:**

1. **Curate Your Social Media Feed:**

social media can be a powerful tool for inspiration and motivation, but it can also contribute to stress and negative self-comparisons. To create a digital environment that supports your wellness journey, be intentional about who you follow. Unfollow or mute accounts that promote unhealthy behaviours or trigger negative emotions, and instead, follow accounts that inspire healthy living, positivity, and personal growth.

2. **Limit Screen Time:**

Excessive screen time, especially before bed, can negatively impact your sleep and overall health. Set boundaries for your digital consumption by limiting screen time, especially on social media and entertainment platforms. Consider implementing a digital detox routine, such as avoiding screens for an hour before bed or setting specific times during the day when you disconnect from technology. This helps reduce mental clutter and promotes a healthier, more balanced lifestyle.

3. **Use Wellness Apps and Tools:**

Technology can also be a powerful ally in your wellness journey. Use apps and tools that support your health goals, such as meditation apps, fitness trackers, or meal planning tools. These resources can help you stay organized, track your progress, and maintain accountability. By choosing apps and tools that align with your wellness objectives, you create a digital environment that actively supports your journey.

**Story Example:**

Jake, a 32-year-old software engineer, found himself feeling overwhelmed and anxious due to the constant barrage of negative news and social media comparisons. He realized that his digital environment was contributing to his stress and decided to make some changes. Jake unfollowed accounts that made him feel inadequate and started following wellness-focused influencers who shared positive, motivating content. He also set a rule to avoid screens for an hour before bed and began using a meditation app to unwind in the evenings. These changes helped Jake create a more positive and supportive digital environment, leading to reduced stress and a greater sense.

# Chapter 7: Decluttering Your Finances— Achieving Financial Freedom

# Section 1: Understanding Financial Clutter—Identifying What's Holding You Back

Financial clutter is more than just the stacks of unopened bills or the disorganized receipts piling up in your drawers. It's the accumulation of disordered and unmanaged financial elements that can create stress, anxiety, and even paralysis when it comes to making financial decisions. Understanding financial clutter requires a deep dive into both the tangible and intangible aspects of your financial life. In this section, we'll explore the various forms of financial clutter, how they affect your well-being, and most importantly, how to identify and start clearing them out.

## What is Financial Clutter?

Financial clutter manifests in various ways, from physical disorganization to emotional and mental blocks that prevent us from achieving financial clarity. It's important to recognize that financial clutter isn't just about having too many things—it's about the psychological and emotional weight these things carry. Whether it's unopened bills, unused subscriptions, or even a lack of financial goals, financial clutter creates confusion and hinders your ability to manage your money effectively.

**Types of Financial Clutter:**

1. **Physical Financial Clutter**: This is the most obvious form of financial clutter and includes things like unfiled paperwork, unopened bills, scattered receipts, and multiple bank accounts. It's easy to accumulate physical financial clutter when you're not consistently organizing or filing your documents. However, physical clutter is just the surface of a deeper issue.

2. **Mental Financial Clutter**: This refers to the overwhelming thoughts and stress related to money management. If you're constantly worried about paying bills, managing debt, or saving for the future, you might be experiencing mental financial clutter. This type of clutter often leads to procrastination, where you put off dealing with financial matters because they feel too overwhelming.

3. **Emotional Financial Clutter**: Emotional attachments can also create financial clutter.

Perhaps you're holding onto investments that aren't performing because of sentimental reasons, or you're overspending as a way to cope with stress. Emotional financial clutter is deeply tied to our beliefs and feelings about money, and it can be the hardest to let go of.

4. **Digital Financial Clutter**: In today's digital age, financial clutter also exists in the form of digital documents, emails, and online accounts. Multiple email accounts filled with financial statements, a cluttered desktop with financial files, or even numerous online subscriptions can create a digital mess that's hard to navigate.

## Why We Accumulate Financial Clutter

To effectively declutter your finances, it's essential to understand why we accumulate financial clutter in the first place. There are several psychological and behavioural factors at play.

**1. Procrastination and Avoidance**: Financial tasks can often feel overwhelming, leading to procrastination. Whether it's avoiding paying bills, delaying the organization of financial documents, or postponing budgeting, procrastination can cause financial clutter to accumulate rapidly.

**2. Emotional Spending**: Emotional spending, often referred to as "retail therapy," can create financial clutter in the form of unnecessary purchases. This can lead to a cycle of spending that clutters both your physical space and financial statements with items and expenses that don't add value to your life.

**3. Lack of Financial Education**: Many people simply haven't been taught how to manage their finances effectively. Without a clear understanding of budgeting, saving, and investing, it's easy to make decisions that contribute to financial disorganization.

**4. Fear and Anxiety**: Fear of making the wrong financial decision can lead to inaction. This inaction can cause financial tasks to pile up, creating clutter that becomes increasingly difficult to manage.

**5. Sentimental Attachment**: Just as with physical objects, we can have sentimental attachments to financial decisions, such as holding onto an underperforming investment because of the emotional significance it holds.

**Story Example:** *Sarah's Story*

Sarah, a 45-year-old marketing executive, always felt overwhelmed by her finances. Despite earning a good salary, she never seemed to have control over her money. Her desk was piled high with unopened bills, and her email inbox was flooded with financial statements and offers from credit card companies. She avoided looking at her bank account because the sight of her balance filled her with anxiety.

After years of this, Sarah decided to make a change. She started by addressing the physical clutter, setting aside a weekend to organize her paperwork and set up a filing system. As she sorted through her documents, she realized that much of her anxiety stemmed from not knowing where she stood financially. This realization led her to tackle the mental and emotional clutter that had been weighing her down.

Sarah began working with a financial advisor who helped her understand her spending habits and set realistic financial goals. Over time, as she gained clarity and control over her finances, her anxiety decreased. Sarah found that by addressing her financial clutter, she was able to regain a sense of peace and confidence in her financial future.

## Practical Steps to Identify Financial Clutter

To begin the process of decluttering your finances, it's important to first identify where the clutter exists in your life. Here are some practical steps to help you get started:

**1. Conduct a Financial Inventory**: Take stock of your financial situation by listing out all your accounts, assets, debts, and recurring expenses. This inventory will give you a clear picture of your financial landscape and help you identify areas of clutter.

**2. Review Your Physical and Digital Spaces**: Go through your physical paperwork and digital files to see what's necessary and what can be discarded or organized. Set up a filing system for important documents and consider going paperless where possible to reduce physical clutter.

**3. Analyse Your Spending Habits**: Review your bank and credit card statements to identify patterns in your spending. Are there subscriptions you're not using? Are you making frequent impulse purchases? Understanding your spending habits will help you see where financial clutter is accumulating.

**4. Set Financial Goals**: Without clear financial goals, it's easy to lose track of your finances. Setting short-term and long-term goals will give you direction and help you stay focused on what's important, reducing the likelihood of financial clutter.

**5. Address Emotional Attachments**: Reflect on any emotional attachments you have to financial decisions. Are there investments you're holding onto for sentimental reasons? Are you avoiding certain financial tasks because they trigger negative emotions? Recognizing these emotional ties can help you make more rational decisions.

**Story Example**: *Mark's Journey*

Mark, a 50-year-old small business owner, struggled with financial clutter for years. His office was filled with boxes of receipts, old contracts, and stacks of unopened mail. Mark's financial disorganization was affecting his business and personal life. He missed important deadlines, paid late fees on bills, and felt constantly stressed about money.

One day, after missing a crucial tax deadline, Mark realized he needed to make a change. He started by hiring an accountant to help him sort through his financial paperwork and set up a system for tracking expenses and income. The accountant also introduced Mark to digital tools that could help him keep his finances organized.

As Mark began to declutter his finances, he noticed a significant reduction in his stress levels. He no longer felt overwhelmed by the piles of paperwork, and he was able to focus more on growing his business. Mark's journey showed him that taking control of his financial clutter was not only possible but also essential for his success.

## The Benefits of Addressing Financial Clutter

Decluttering your finances can have a profound impact on your overall well-being. Here are some of the benefits you can expect:

1. **Reduced Stress and Anxiety**: When your finances are organized and under control, you'll experience less stress and anxiety. You'll have a clear understanding of your financial situation, which can provide peace of mind.

2. **Improved Financial Health**: By eliminating financial clutter, you'll be better able to manage your money, pay down debt, and save for the future. This leads to improved financial health and greater financial security.

**3. Enhanced Decision-Making**: With less financial clutter, you'll have the clarity needed to make informed decisions. Whether it's investing, budgeting, or planning for retirement, you'll be able to approach your finances with confidence.

**4. Greater Focus on Goals**: Decluttering your finances allows you to focus on your financial goals without the distraction of unnecessary clutter. This focus can help you achieve your goals more quickly and effectively.

**5. Increased Productivity**: A decluttered financial life can lead to increased productivity in other areas of your life. With less mental clutter, you'll be able to concentrate better on your work and personal projects.

# Section 2: Simplifying Your Finances—Strategies for Streamlining and Organizing

Simplifying your finances is about more than just reducing the number of accounts you have or paying off debts. It's about creating a financial system that is easy to manage, aligns with your life goals, and minimizes the stress and confusion that often come with financial management. In this section, we'll explore practical strategies for streamlining and organizing your finances, making it easier for you to maintain control and achieve financial freedom.

## 1. Consolidating Accounts and Debts

One of the first steps to simplifying your finances is to consolidate where possible. Many people have multiple bank accounts, credit cards, and loans, which can lead to confusion and missed payments. By consolidating these accounts and debts, you can reduce the number of financial elements you need to manage, making it easier to stay on top of your finances.

**Consolidating Bank Accounts:** If you have multiple bank accounts at different institutions, consider consolidating them into one or two accounts at a single bank. This makes it easier to track your income and expenses, reduces the risk of overdrafts, and can help you avoid unnecessary fees. For example, you might choose to keep a primary checking account for daily transactions and a savings account for your emergency fund and long-term savings.

**Debt Consolidation:** Debt consolidation involves combining multiple debts, such as credit card balances, into a single loan with a lower interest rate. This can simplify your repayment process by giving you just one monthly payment to manage instead of several. Additionally, consolidating debt can save you money on interest and help you pay off your debt faster.

**Story Example:** *Jessica's Experience with Debt Consolidation*

Jessica, a 35-year-old nurse, found herself struggling to keep up with her financial obligations. She had three credit cards with high balances and interest rates, as well as a car loan and a student loan. The sheer number of payments she had to make each month left her feeling overwhelmed and stressed.

After speaking with a financial advisor, Jessica decided to consolidate her credit card debt into a personal loan with a lower interest rate. This move not only reduced the amount of interest she was paying but also simplified her finances by turning three separate payments into one. With her finances streamlined, Jessica was able to focus on paying off her debts more aggressively, and within two years, she was debt-free.

## 2. Automating Your Finances

Automation is a powerful tool for simplifying your finances. By automating your bill payments, savings, and investments, you can reduce the risk of late payments, ensure you're consistently saving, and eliminate the need to manually manage every aspect of your financial life.

**Automating Bill Payments:** Setting up automatic payments for your bills ensures that you never miss a payment, which can save you from late fees and damage to your credit score. Most banks and service providers offer options to set up recurring payments directly from your bank account or credit card. Just be sure to monitor your account regularly to ensure you have enough funds to cover these automatic payments.

**Automating Savings:** One of the most effective ways to build savings is to automate the process. Set up a direct deposit from your paycheck into a savings account, so a portion of your income is saved before you even have a chance to spend it. You can also automate contributions to retirement accounts, such as a 401(k) or IRA, ensuring you're consistently working toward your long-term financial goals.

**Automating Investments:** Automating your investments can help you build wealth over time without needing to actively manage your portfolio. Many investment platforms allow you to set up recurring contributions to your investment accounts. This strategy, known as dollar-cost averaging, helps you invest consistently, regardless of market conditions, and can reduce the emotional impact of market volatility.

**Story Example:** *David's Path to Consistent Saving*

David, a 28-year-old software engineer, struggled with saving money. Despite earning a good salary, he often found himself spending more than he planned and saving very little. After attending a personal finance workshop, David decided to automate his savings. He set up his direct deposit to allocate 10% of his paycheck to a high-yield savings account and another 5% to his retirement account.

With his savings automated, David no longer had to rely on his willpower to save money. Over time, he saw his savings grow steadily, giving him a sense of security and confidence in his financial future. The automation made saving effortless and helped David stay on track with his financial goals.

## 3. Simplifying Your Budget

Budgeting is a fundamental aspect of financial management, but it doesn't have to be complicated. A simplified budget can help you manage your money effectively without requiring hours of tracking and categorizing every expense.

**The 50/30/20 Budgeting Rule:** One of the simplest and most effective budgeting methods is the 50/30/20 rule. This rule divides your after-tax income into three categories:

- **50% for needs:** Essential expenses like housing, utilities, groceries, and transportation.

- **30% for wants:** Discretionary spending on things like dining out, entertainment, and hobbies.

- **20% for savings and debt repayment:** Contributions to savings accounts, retirement funds, and debt payments.

This approach provides a clear structure for managing your money while allowing flexibility within each category. It's particularly useful for those who find detailed budgeting overwhelming.

**Using Budgeting Apps:** Budgeting apps can simplify the process by tracking your expenses, categorizing them automatically, and providing insights into your spending habits. Apps like Mint, YNAB (You Need A Budget), and PocketGuard can link to your bank accounts and credit cards, giving you a real-time view of your finances. These tools can help you stay on top of your budget without the need for manual tracking.

**Story Example:** *Maria's Simplified Budgeting Journey*

Maria, a 32-year-old teacher, found traditional budgeting methods too time-consuming and stressful. She tried using spreadsheets to track her expenses, but it felt like a chore, and she often fell behind. After researching different budgeting methods, Maria decided to try the 50/30/20 rule.

By dividing her income into three simple categories, Maria found budgeting much easier to manage. She didn't have to worry about tracking every penny, and she enjoyed the flexibility the rule provided. Maria also started using a budgeting app that linked to her bank account, giving her an overview of her spending with minimal effort. The simplified approach helped Maria regain control of her finances without feeling overwhelmed.

## 4. Decluttering Your Financial Records

Organizing your financial records is crucial for managing your finances efficiently. Whether it's physical paperwork or digital documents, keeping your records in order can save you time, reduce stress, and help you avoid costly mistakes.

**Organizing Physical Records:** Start by sorting through your physical financial documents. Shred or discard outdated and unnecessary paperwork, such as old bank statements, paid bills, and expired insurance policies. Create a filing system for the remaining documents, organizing them into categories like taxes, insurance, bank accounts, and investments. Use labelled folders or a filing cabinet to keep everything in order and easily accessible.

**Digitizing Financial Documents:** Consider going paperless by digitizing your financial documents. Use a scanner or smartphone app to create digital copies of important paperwork, and store them in a secure, organized digital filing system. Cloud storage services like Google Drive, Dropbox, or OneDrive can keep your files safe and accessible from anywhere. Be sure to back up your digital records regularly to avoid data loss.

**Managing Digital Financial Information:** Your digital financial clutter can be just as overwhelming as physical clutter. Start by organizing your email inbox, creating folders for different types of financial correspondence, such as bills, bank statements, and investment updates. Unsubscribe from unnecessary financial newsletters and promotional emails to reduce clutter in your inbox.

**Story Example:** *Tom's Transformation from Chaos to Order*

Tom, a 45-year-old contractor, was drowning in financial paperwork. His desk was cluttered with bills, tax forms, and receipts, and he often struggled to find important documents when he needed them. After missing a tax filing deadline, Tom decided it was time to get organized.

Tom began by sorting through his piles of paperwork, discarding what was no longer needed and organizing the rest into labelled folders. He also decided to go paperless, scanning important documents and storing them in a cloud-based filing system. With his financial records organized, Tom felt a sense of relief and newfound control over his finances. He was no longer stressed about finding documents, and he could focus on growing his business.

## 5. Reviewing and Simplifying Subscriptions and Recurring Expenses

Recurring expenses, such as subscriptions and memberships, can easily clutter your financial life and drain your budget without you even realizing it. Simplifying these expenses can free up money for more important financial goals.

**Conduct a Subscription Audit:** Start by reviewing all your subscriptions and recurring expenses. This includes streaming services, gym memberships, software subscriptions, and any other recurring charges on your bank or credit card statements. Identify which subscriptions you truly use and value, and cancel those that are no longer necessary.

**Bundling Services:** In some cases, bundling services can save you money and reduce the number of bills you need to manage. For example, many streaming services offer bundle deals, or you might be able to combine your internet and phone services into a single bill. This can simplify your financial life by consolidating multiple expenses into one.

**Story Example:** *Linda's Subscription Cleanup*

Linda, a 40-year-old graphic designer, realized she was spending hundreds of dollars a month on subscriptions she rarely used. Between streaming services, digital magazines, and software subscriptions, her budget was stretched thin, and she often struggled to save money.

After conducting a subscription audit, Linda was shocked at how much she was spending on services she barely used. She decided to cancel several subscriptions and downgrade others to lower-cost plans. This simple cleanup freed up a significant amount of money each month, which Linda redirected toward her emergency fund and retirement savings. Simplifying her recurring expenses gave Linda more financial flexibility and peace of mind.

# Section 3: Building a Sustainable Financial Future—Long-Term Habits for Financial Freedom

Creating a sustainable financial future requires more than just getting your finances in order today; it's about developing habits that will keep you on track for the long haul. Financial freedom is the result of consistent, disciplined habits that build wealth, reduce debt, and prepare you for life's uncertainties. In this section, we'll explore the key habits that can help you maintain financial health over the long term, providing you with security and peace of mind.

## 1. Living Below Your Means

One of the most fundamental habits for achieving financial freedom is living below your means. This means spending less than you earn and avoiding lifestyle inflation, which occurs when your spending increases in proportion to your income.

**Practical Advice:**

- **Track Your Spending:** Keep a detailed record of your income and expenses. This can help you identify areas where you may be overspending and opportunities to cut back.

- **Set a Budget:** Establish a realistic budget that aligns with your financial goals. Allocate a portion of your income to savings and investments before considering discretionary spending.

- **Avoid Lifestyle Inflation:** As your income grows, resist the temptation to increase your spending proportionally. Instead, use the extra income to boost your savings, pay off debt, or invest in your future.

**Story Example:** *Sarah's Journey to Financial Independence*

Sarah, a 30-year-old marketing manager, had always dreamed of achieving financial independence. Despite earning a good salary, she found herself living paycheck to paycheck, with little to show for her hard work. Realizing that her spending habits were holding her back, Sarah decided to make a change.

She started by tracking her expenses and was shocked to discover how much she was spending on dining out, shopping, and other non-essential items. Sarah created a budget that prioritized her financial goals, including saving for a home and building an emergency fund. By living below her means, Sarah was able to save a significant portion of her income each month. Over time, her savings grew, and she became more confident in her financial future.

## 2. Consistent Saving and Investing

Building a sustainable financial future requires consistent saving and investing. The earlier you start, the more time your money has to grow through the power of compound interest. Whether you're saving for a specific goal or building a retirement nest egg, making regular contributions is key.

**Practical Advice:**

- **Pay Yourself First:** Automate your savings by setting up a direct deposit into a savings or investment account. This ensures you're consistently saving a portion of your income before you have a chance to spend it.

- **Diversify Your Investments:** Spread your investments across different asset classes, such as stocks, bonds, and real estate, to reduce risk and increase the potential for growth. Consider working with a financial advisor to develop an investment strategy that aligns with your goals and risk tolerance.

- **Increase Contributions Over Time:** As your income grows, gradually increase the amount you save and invest. This can help you build wealth more quickly and take advantage of compound interest.

**Story Example:** *John's Commitment to Consistent Investing*

John, a 40-year-old engineer, knew that saving for retirement was important, but he had always found it difficult to set aside money consistently. After attending a financial planning seminar, John decided to automate his retirement savings. He set up a direct deposit that automatically transferred 15% of his paycheck into his 401(k) account each month.

John also diversified his investments, spreading them across stocks, bonds, and mutual funds. Over the years,

John increased his contributions as his income grew, and he regularly reviewed his investment portfolio to ensure it remained aligned with his long-term goals. By consistently saving and investing, John was able to build a substantial retirement fund, giving him the confidence to retire comfortably in his 60s.

## 3. Managing Debt Wisely

Debt can be a significant obstacle to financial freedom, but managing it wisely can help you stay on the path to a sustainable financial future. This involves understanding the difference between good debt (like a mortgage or student loan) and bad debt (like high-interest credit card debt) and making strategic decisions about when and how to borrow.

**Practical Advice:**

- **Prioritize High-Interest Debt:** Focus on paying off high-interest debt, such as credit card balances, as quickly as possible. The longer you carry high-interest debt, the more it costs you in the long run.

- **Use Debt Strategically:** Not all debt is bad. For example, taking out a mortgage to buy a home or a student loan to further your education can be a wise investment in your future. The key is to borrow only what you can afford to repay and to ensure that the debt aligns with your long-term financial goals.

- **Avoid Unnecessary Debt:** Resist the temptation to take on debt for non-essential purchases, such as luxury items or vacations. If you can't afford to pay for something outright, consider whether it's truly necessary.

**Story Example:** *Emily's Strategy for Managing Debt*

Emily, a 27-year-old teacher, was burdened by student loans and credit card debt. The stress of managing multiple debts was overwhelming, and she worried that she would never be able to achieve financial freedom. After seeking advice from a financial counsellor, Emily developed a plan to tackle her debt.

She started by focusing on her credit card debt, which had the highest interest rate. Emily used the debt snowball method, paying off the smallest balances first while making minimum payments on the larger debts. As she paid off each credit card, she felt a sense of accomplishment and used the momentum to tackle her student loans next. By managing her debt wisely and avoiding new debt, Emily was able to regain control of her finances and move closer to her goal of financial freedom.

## 4. Building an Emergency Fund

An emergency fund is a crucial component of a sustainable financial future. It provides a financial safety net in case of unexpected expenses, such as medical emergencies, car repairs, or job loss. Having an emergency fund can help you avoid going into debt when life's surprises arise.

**Practical Advice:**

- **Set a Goal:** Aim to save at least three to six months' worth of living expenses in your emergency fund. This amount should cover essential costs like rent or mortgage payments, utilities, groceries, and insurance.

- **Keep It Accessible:** Your emergency fund should be kept in a liquid account, such as a high-yield savings account, where it can be easily accessed in an emergency. Avoid investing this money in stocks or other volatile assets, as you want to ensure it's available when you need it.

- **Start Small and Build:** If saving three to six months' worth of expenses seems daunting, start with a smaller goal, such as $1,000. Once you reach that milestone, continue building your fund until you reach your target.

**Story Example:** *Laura's Lifesaving Emergency Fund*

Laura, a 38-year-old freelance graphic designer, understood the importance of having an emergency fund. With an unpredictable income, she knew that having a financial cushion was essential to weathering the ups and downs of her career. Laura set a goal to save six months' worth of living expenses and began contributing a portion of her income to her emergency fund each month.

When the COVID-19 pandemic hit, many of Laura's clients cut back on projects, and her income dropped significantly. However, thanks to her emergency fund, Laura was able to cover her living expenses without going into debt. Her financial cushion gave her peace of mind during a difficult time, allowing her to focus on finding new clients and rebuilding her business.

## 5. Planning for Retirement

Planning for retirement is a critical aspect of building a sustainable financial future. The earlier you start, the more time your investments have to grow, and the less you'll need to save each year to reach your retirement goals.

**Practical Advice:**

- **Calculate Your Retirement Needs:** Determine how much money you'll need to retire comfortably. Consider factors such as your desired retirement age, lifestyle expectations, and potential healthcare costs. Online retirement calculators can help you estimate your needs based on your current savings and investment strategy.

- **Maximize Retirement Contributions:** Take full advantage of retirement accounts like 401(k)s, IRAs, or Roth IRAs. If your employer offers a 401(k) match, contribute enough to get the full match, as this is essentially free money. The more you contribute now, the less you'll need to save later.

- **Adjust Your Plan as Needed:** Life is unpredictable, and your retirement plan may need to change over time. Regularly review your retirement accounts and make adjustments as needed to stay on track with your goals.

**Story Example:** *Mark's Retirement Planning Success*

Mark, a 50-year-old accountant, had been contributing to his 401(k) since he started working in his 20s. However, as he approached retirement age, he realized that his savings might not be enough to support the lifestyle he wanted in retirement. Mark decided to meet with a financial planner to reassess his retirement goals.

After reviewing his finances, Mark increased his 401(k) contributions and opened a Roth IRA to take advantage of tax-free growth. He also adjusted his investment strategy to balance growth potential with risk management as he neared retirement. By planning ahead and making strategic adjustments, Mark was able to secure a comfortable retirement and enjoy the financial freedom he had worked so hard to achieve.

## 6. Continuously Educating Yourself

Financial literacy is an ongoing journey. Staying informed about personal finance, investing, and economic trends can help you make better financial decisions and adapt to changes in your financial situation.

### Practical Advice:

- **Read and Learn:** Make a habit of reading books, articles, and blogs about personal finance and investing. Consider following reputable financial experts and subscribing to financial newsletters to stay updated on the latest trends.

- **Attend Workshops and Seminars:** Participate in financial workshops, seminars, or webinars to expand your knowledge. These events often cover a wide range of topics, from budgeting and saving to investing and retirement planning.

- **Consult with Professionals:** Don't hesitate to seek advice from financial professionals, such as financial planners or tax advisors. They can provide personalized guidance and help you make informed decisions based on your specific circumstances.

**Story Example:** *Rachel's Commitment to Financial Education*

Rachel, a 35-year-old small business owner, realized that her lack of financial knowledge was holding her back from achieving her goals. Determined to improve her financial literacy, Rachel began reading books on personal finance, listening to financial podcasts, and attending local workshops.

As Rachel's knowledge grew, so did her confidence in managing her finances. She learned how to create a more effective budget, invest wisely, and plan for the future. By continuously educating herself, Rachel was able to take control of her financial life and build a sustainable future for herself and her family.

# Chapter 8: Decluttering for Success—Amplifying Your Productivity and Achievements

# Section 1: The Link Between Clutter and Productivity—Understanding How Clutter Impacts Your Performance

Clutter is more than just an aesthetic problem—it can significantly affect your productivity and overall performance. When your environment is cluttered, it can lead to distractions, increased stress, and a decrease in efficiency. Understanding how clutter impacts your productivity is the first step toward creating a more organized, focused, and effective workspace. This section will explore the link between clutter and productivity, offering practical advice and real-life examples to help you recognize and address the clutter in your life.

## 1. The Science Behind Clutter and Productivity

Numerous studies have demonstrated that clutter can have a profound impact on your cognitive abilities and productivity. The brain is wired to seek order and organization, and when your environment is cluttered, it can lead to mental overload. This phenomenon is known as "visual clutter," where the presence of too many objects in your field of vision competes for your attention and reduces your ability to focus.

**Practical Advice:**

- **Minimize Visual Distractions:** Keep your workspace as tidy as possible. Limit the number of items on your desk to only those that are essential for your work. Store other items in drawers or cabinets to reduce visual clutter.

- **Use the "One-Touch Rule":** When handling paperwork or other items, try to deal with them immediately rather than setting them aside for later. This practice can help prevent clutter from accumulating and keeps your workspace organized.

- **Create Designated Spaces:** Assign specific places for items you use frequently, such as pens, notepads, and files. When everything has a place, it's easier to maintain order and avoid clutter.

**Story Example:** *Michael's Transformation from Chaos to Clarity*

Michael, a graphic designer, found that his cluttered workspace was making it difficult for him to concentrate and meet deadlines. His desk was covered with sketches, design tools, coffee mugs, and personal items. The visual clutter made it challenging for him to focus on his work, and he often felt overwhelmed.

After learning about the impact of clutter on productivity, Michael decided to declutter his workspace. He started by clearing everything off his desk and only returned the items he used daily. He stored the rest in drawers and organized his files digitally. The transformation was immediate—Michael found that his ability to concentrate improved, and he was able to work more efficiently. The clarity in his workspace led to clarity in his mind, boosting his creativity and productivity.

## 2. Clutter and Decision Fatigue

Decision fatigue occurs when your brain becomes tired from making too many decisions, leading to poor choices and decreased productivity. Clutter can contribute to decision fatigue by overwhelming you with too many options and distractions. When your workspace is cluttered, you may find yourself constantly deciding where to put things, what to prioritize, or how to navigate through the mess—using up valuable mental energy that could be better spent on more important tasks.

**Practical Advice:**

- **Simplify Your Environment:** Reduce the number of items in your workspace to minimize the decisions you need to make. For example, keep only one or two pens on your desk instead of an entire collection. Streamlining your environment can help reduce decision fatigue.

- **Implement a Routine:** Establish a daily routine for organizing your workspace. Spend a few minutes at the end of each day tidying up, so you start the next day with a clean, clutter-free environment. This habit can help prevent clutter from accumulating and reduce the number of decisions you need to make.

- **Prioritize Tasks:** Use a to-do list or a task management system to prioritize your work. By having a clear plan for your day, you can avoid the mental strain of constantly deciding what to do next, allowing you to focus on completing tasks more efficiently.

**Story Example:** *Emma's Battle with Decision Fatigue*

Emma, a marketing manager, struggled with decision fatigue due to the constant clutter in her office. Her desk was filled with papers, marketing materials, and personal items, and every day she spent precious time deciding where to put things or what to tackle next. This constant decision-making drained her mental energy, leaving her feeling exhausted by midday.

Determined to improve her productivity, Emma decided to declutter her workspace. She simplified her desk setup, keeping only the essentials within reach. Emma also developed a daily routine of organizing her desk at the end of each day, so she could start the next morning with a clear mind. With fewer decisions to make about her environment, Emma found that she had more mental energy to focus on her work, resulting in better performance and less stress.

## 3. Clutter and Stress

Clutter can be a significant source of stress, which in turn can negatively affect your productivity. When your environment is disorganized, it can create a sense of chaos and anxiety, making it difficult to focus on your work. This stress can lead to procrastination, as you may feel overwhelmed by the thought of tackling tasks in a cluttered space.

**Practical Advice:**

- **Declutter Regularly:** Make decluttering a regular part of your routine. Set aside time each week to go through your workspace and remove unnecessary items. This practice can help prevent clutter from building up and reduce the stress associated with a disorganized environment.

- **Create a Calming Workspace:** Incorporate elements into your workspace that promote a sense of calm and focus. For example, you might add a small plant, use soft lighting, or play soothing background music. A calming environment can help counteract the stress caused by clutter and improve your productivity.

- **Practice Mindfulness:** Mindfulness techniques, such as deep breathing or meditation, can help you manage stress and stay focused in a cluttered environment. Taking a few minutes to clear your mind can make it easier to tackle tasks and maintain productivity, even when your surroundings are less than ideal.

**Story Example:** *Lisa's Journey to a Stress-Free Workspace*

Lisa, a freelance writer, often found herself feeling anxious and stressed in her cluttered home office. The piles of papers, books, and office supplies made it difficult for her to concentrate, and she often procrastinated on her writing projects. The clutter was not only affecting her productivity but also her mental health.

Realizing the impact that clutter was having on her well-being, Lisa decided to take action. She began by decluttering her office, getting rid of items she no longer needed, and organizing the rest into labeled bins and folders. She also added a small plant and a calming picture to her desk to create a more peaceful environment.

As the clutter disappeared, so did Lisa's stress. She found it easier to focus on her writing, and her productivity soared. Lisa's newfound clarity in her workspace led to a significant improvement in her mental health and overall well-being.

## 4. The Impact of Digital Clutter

In today's digital age, clutter isn't limited to physical spaces—digital clutter can also have a profound impact on your productivity. Digital clutter includes things like a cluttered email inbox, disorganized files on your computer, and an overwhelming number of apps on your phone. Just like physical clutter, digital clutter can lead to distractions, stress, and decreased efficiency.

**Practical Advice:**

- **Organize Your Digital Files:** Create a clear and logical folder structure on your computer for your documents, images, and other files. Regularly review and delete files you no longer need to keep your digital workspace organized.

- **Manage Your Email Inbox:** Implement an email management system, such as creating folders for different types of emails and using filters to automatically sort incoming messages. Aim to achieve "inbox zero" by regularly reviewing and responding to emails, then filing or deleting them as necessary.

- **Limit Digital Distractions:** Reduce the number of apps and notifications on your phone and computer. Turn off non-essential notifications, and uninstall apps you no longer use. By minimizing digital distractions, you can stay focused and improve your productivity.

**Story Example:** *Tom's Digital Declutter Success*

Tom, a software developer, found that digital clutter was taking a toll on his productivity. His email inbox was overflowing with unread messages, his computer desktop was covered with files, and his phone was filled with apps he rarely used. The constant barrage of notifications and the difficulty in finding important files made it hard for Tom to focus on his work.

Recognizing the need for a change, Tom decided to declutter his digital life. He started by organizing his computer files into clearly labelled folders, deleting unnecessary files, and backing up important documents. Tom also implemented a system for managing his email, creating folders for different projects and setting aside time each day to process new messages. Finally, he reduced the number of apps on his phone and turned off non-essential notifications.

The results were immediate—Tom found that he was able to focus more easily, complete tasks more efficiently, and feel less overwhelmed by his digital environment. By decluttering his digital life, Tom was able to regain control over his productivity and reduce the stress that had been holding him back.

## 5. Clutter and Creativity

Clutter doesn't just affect your ability to focus—it can also stifle your creativity. A cluttered environment can make it difficult to think clearly and come up with new ideas. On the other hand, a clean and organized space can inspire creativity and help you approach problems with a fresh perspective.

**Practical Advice:**

- **Create a Dedicated Creative Space:** If possible, designate a specific area in your home or office for creative work. Keep this space free from clutter and distractions, and fill it with items that inspire you, such as art, books, or nature elements.

- **Declutter Your Mind:** In addition to decluttering your physical space, take steps to clear your mind as well. This might include journaling, meditating, or going for a walk to clear your thoughts and make space for new ideas.

- **Embrace Minimalism:** Sometimes less is more. Consider adopting a minimalist approach to your workspace, removing all but the most essential items. This can help you focus on your creative work without being distracted by unnecessary clutter.

**Story Example:** *Sarah's Creative Revival*

Sarah, a freelance artist, found herself in a creative slump. Her studio was filled with unfinished projects, art supplies scattered everywhere, and personal items that had no place in her creative space. The clutter was overwhelming, and Sarah found it hard to tap into her creativity.

Determined to reignite her creative spark, Sarah decided to declutter her studio. She started by clearing out everything that wasn't related to her art, organizing her supplies, and creating a clean, open space where she could work. She also set aside time each day to meditate and clear her mind before starting her creative projects.

The difference was like night and day—Sarah's creativity returned in full force, and she was able to complete projects with a renewed sense of passion and inspiration. By decluttering her space and her mind, Sarah was able to unleash her creative potential and take her art to new heights.

# Section 2: Streamlining Your Workflow—Practical Strategies for Enhancing Efficiency

Streamlining your workflow is essential for maximizing efficiency, reducing stress, and achieving your goals more effectively. A well-organized workflow not only saves time but also enhances your ability to focus and produce high-quality work. This section will provide practical strategies for enhancing efficiency, offering real-world examples and actionable advice to help you create a smoother, more productive workflow.

## 1. Prioritization—Focusing on What Matters Most

One of the most effective ways to streamline your workflow is to prioritize your tasks. Not all tasks are created equal—some are crucial to achieving your goals, while others are less important. By identifying and focusing on high-priority tasks, you can ensure that your time and energy are spent on activities that have the greatest impact.

**Practical Advice:**

- **Use the Eisenhower Matrix:** The Eisenhower Matrix is a tool that helps you categorize tasks into four quadrants: urgent and important, important but not urgent, urgent but not important, and neither urgent nor important. This method allows you to prioritize tasks based on their importance and urgency, helping you focus on what truly matters.

- **Set Daily Priorities:** At the beginning of each day, identify the top three tasks that you must accomplish. These tasks should be aligned with your long-term goals and have a significant impact on your work. By setting clear priorities, you can avoid getting sidetracked by less important activities.

- **Limit Your To-Do List:** A lengthy to-do list can be overwhelming and counterproductive. Instead, create a short list of high-priority tasks for each day. Focus on completing these tasks before moving on to anything else. This approach ensures that you make meaningful progress on your most important work.

**Story Example:** *James' Journey to Prioritization*

James, a project manager, often found himself overwhelmed by the sheer number of tasks on his to-do list. He would start his day with the intention of being productive, but by mid-afternoon, he was drowning in a sea of emails, meetings, and minor tasks that seemed to take up all his time. Despite working long hours, James struggled to make meaningful progress on his projects.

Realizing that his current approach wasn't sustainable, James decided to try the Eisenhower Matrix. He categorized his tasks based on their importance and urgency, and to his surprise, he discovered that many of the tasks he had been focusing on were neither urgent nor important. By shifting his focus to the tasks that truly mattered, James was able to streamline his workflow, reduce stress, and achieve better results. His productivity improved, and he was finally able to make progress on his key projects.

## 2. Time Management—Maximizing Your Efficiency

Effective time management is crucial for streamlining your workflow. By managing your time wisely, you can accomplish more in less time and avoid the pitfalls of procrastination and time-wasting activities. Time management strategies help you stay focused, organized, and productive throughout the day.

**Practical Advice:**

- **The Pomodoro Technique:** The Pomodoro Technique involves working in short, focused bursts of 25 minutes, followed by a 5-minute break. After four Pomodoros, take a longer break of 15-30 minutes. This method helps you maintain concentration and prevent burnout, making it easier to complete tasks efficiently.

- **Batching Similar Tasks:** Grouping similar tasks together can save time and reduce cognitive switching costs. For example, set aside specific times for checking and responding to emails, making phone calls, or working on related projects. Batching tasks reduces the mental effort required to switch between different types of work and increases efficiency.

- **Time Blocking:** Time blocking involves scheduling specific blocks of time for different tasks or activities. By allocating dedicated time for each task, you can ensure that you stay on track and avoid multitasking. Time blocking also helps you create a structured day, making it easier to manage your time and stay productive.

**Story Example:** *Sophie's Time Management Transformation*

Sophie, a freelance writer, struggled with managing her time effectively. She often found herself working late into the night, trying to meet deadlines after spending too much time on non-essential tasks during the day. The lack of structure in her workday made it difficult for her to stay focused and productive.

Determined to take control of her time, Sophie decided to implement the Pomodoro Technique. She began breaking her work into 25-minute intervals, with short breaks in between. This method helped her stay focused and motivated, allowing her to accomplish more in less time. Sophie also started batching similar tasks together, such as researching for multiple articles in one session, which saved her time and mental energy. By adopting these time management strategies, Sophie was able to streamline her workflow, meet deadlines with ease, and create a better work-life balance.

## 3. Simplifying Processes—Eliminating Inefficiencies

Simplifying processes is another key strategy for streamlining your workflow. Complex, cumbersome processes can slow you down and create unnecessary obstacles. By identifying and eliminating inefficiencies, you can create a smoother, more efficient workflow that allows you to focus on what really matters.

**Practical Advice:**

- **Automate Repetitive Tasks:** Automation is a powerful tool for streamlining your workflow. Identify repetitive tasks that can be automated, such as data entry, email responses, or scheduling. Tools like email filters, calendar apps, and project management software can help you automate these tasks, freeing up time for more important work.

- **Standardize Workflows:** Creating standardized workflows for recurring tasks can help you maintain consistency and efficiency. Document the steps involved in each process and use templates or checklists to ensure that tasks are completed in the same way every time. Standardization reduces the need for decision-making and minimizes the risk of errors.

- **Review and Optimize Processes Regularly:** Regularly reviewing your workflows allows you to identify areas for improvement. Take the time to evaluate each process and look for ways to simplify or streamline it. This might involve eliminating unnecessary steps, consolidating tasks, or adopting new tools or technologies.

**Story Example:** *Emily's Workflow Optimization*

Emily, an operations manager at a small business, noticed that her team was spending a lot of time on repetitive tasks, such as entering data into spreadsheets and sending routine emails. The inefficiencies in their processes were causing delays and reducing overall productivity.

To address this issue, Emily decided to automate as many tasks as possible. She implemented software that automatically pulled data from various sources and populated the necessary spreadsheets. She also set up email templates and automated responses for common inquiries. Additionally, Emily worked with her team to standardize their workflows, creating templates and checklists for recurring tasks.

The impact was immediate—by eliminating inefficiencies and automating repetitive tasks, Emily's team was able to focus on more valuable work. Productivity improved, and the team was able to complete projects more quickly and accurately. Emily's efforts to streamline their workflow paid off, creating a more efficient and effective work environment.

## 4. Delegation—Leveraging the Power of Teamwork

Delegation is a critical aspect of streamlining your workflow, especially if you're in a leadership position. Trying to do everything yourself can lead to burnout and inefficiency. By delegating tasks to others, you can focus on your core responsibilities and leverage the strengths of your team members.

**Practical Advice:**

- **Identify Tasks for Delegation:** Not every task needs to be done by you. Identify tasks that can be delegated to others, such as routine administrative work, data entry, or tasks that fall within your team members' expertise. Delegating these tasks allows you to focus on higher-level work that requires your unique skills and knowledge.

- **Empower Your Team:** Effective delegation involves more than just assigning tasks—it's about empowering your team to take ownership of their work. Provide clear instructions, set expectations, and offer support as needed. Trust your team to deliver results, and give them the autonomy to make decisions within their areas of responsibility.

- **Follow Up and Provide Feedback:** Delegation doesn't end when you assign a task. Follow up regularly to ensure that the task is progressing as expected, and provide constructive feedback to help your team improve. Regular communication ensures that delegated tasks are completed on time and to the desired standard.

**Story Example:** *Rachel's Delegation Success*

Rachel, a marketing director at a growing company, found herself overwhelmed with responsibilities. She was handling everything from strategic planning to social media management, leaving her little time for high-level decision-making. The lack of delegation was not only affecting her productivity but also the overall performance of her team.

Recognizing the need for change, Rachel decided to delegate more tasks to her team. She identified tasks that could be handled by others, such as content creation, social media scheduling, and data analysis. Rachel empowered her team by providing clear instructions and the necessary resources to succeed. She also made it a point to check in regularly and offer feedback to ensure that the work met her standards.

The results were remarkable—Rachel's team members took ownership of their tasks and delivered high-quality work. With more time to focus on strategic planning and leadership, Rachel was able to drive the company's marketing efforts forward. By delegating effectively, she not only improved her own productivity but also strengthened her team's performance.

## 5. Continuous Improvement—Adapting and Evolving Your Workflow

Streamlining your workflow is not a one-time effort—it's an ongoing process that requires continuous improvement. As your work evolves, so too should your workflows. By regularly assessing and adapting your processes, you can stay ahead of the curve and maintain a high level of efficiency.

**Practical Advice:**

- **Regularly Review Your Workflow:** Set aside time each month or quarter to review your workflow and identify areas for improvement. Look for bottlenecks, inefficiencies, or tasks that could be automated or delegated. Regular reviews help you stay proactive and make necessary adjustments before problems arise.

- **Seek Feedback:** Don't hesitate to ask for feedback from colleagues, team members, or supervisors. They may have valuable insights into how your workflow could be improved. Collaborative feedback can lead to new ideas and solutions that you might not have considered on your own.

- **Stay Open to Change:** The most efficient workflows are those that can adapt to changing circumstances. Stay open to new tools, technologies, and methods that could enhance your efficiency. Embrace change as an opportunity to refine and optimize your workflow.

**Story Example:** *John's Journey to Continuous Improvement*

John, a software developer, was known for his meticulous approach to work. However, as his projects grew more complex, he realized that his workflow needed to evolve. The tools and processes that had served him well in the past were no longer sufficient to handle the demands of his current projects.

John began by reviewing his workflow and identifying areas for improvement. He sought feedback from his colleagues and explored new tools that could help him work more efficiently. After some trial and error, John found a project management software that streamlined his workflow and allowed him to track his progress more effectively.

By embracing continuous improvement, John was able to adapt to the changing demands of his work. His productivity increased, and he was able to deliver high-quality results more quickly. John's commitment to refining his workflow paid off, allowing him to stay ahead in his field.

# Section 3: Setting and Achieving Goals—How Decluttering Can Drive Your Success

Decluttering is more than just clearing out physical spaces; it's about making room for what truly matters in your life. By removing unnecessary distractions and focusing on your goals, you can create a clear path toward success. This section will explore how decluttering can be a powerful tool in setting and achieving your goals, offering practical advice and real-world stories to illustrate the impact of a clutter-free life on your journey to success.

## 1. The Connection Between Clutter and Goal Achievement

Clutter isn't just about physical objects—it can also manifest as mental and emotional clutter, all of which can interfere with your ability to set and achieve goals. Clutter creates noise in your environment and mind, making it difficult to focus on what you truly want to accomplish.

**Practical Advice:**

- **Identify Your Clutter Sources:** Before setting goals, take a step back and identify the sources of clutter in your life. This could include a disorganized workspace, a chaotic schedule, or negative thoughts that cloud your mind. Understanding where clutter exists allows you to address it directly and create a more focused environment.

- **Simplify Your Environment:** Start by decluttering your physical space. A clean and organized environment can greatly enhance your ability to concentrate and think clearly. For example, clearing your desk of unnecessary items can help you focus better on the task at hand, reducing distractions and improving productivity.

- **Declutter Your Mind:** Mental clutter, such as overthinking, self-doubt, and unresolved emotions, can be just as obstructive as physical clutter. Practice mindfulness techniques, such as meditation or journaling, to clear your mind and create mental space for goal-setting and achievement.

**Story Example:** *Sarah's Mental Decluttering Journey*

Sarah, a graphic designer, found herself struggling to meet deadlines and achieve her career goals. Despite being talented and passionate about her work, she often felt overwhelmed and unfocused. After some reflection, Sarah realized that her cluttered mind was the root of the problem. She was constantly juggling multiple thoughts and worries, which left little room for creative thinking.

To address this, Sarah started a daily journaling practice. Each morning, she would spend 10 minutes writing down her thoughts, worries, and ideas. This simple practice helped her clear her mind and prioritize her tasks for the day. Over time, Sarah noticed a significant improvement in her ability to focus on her goals. Her creativity flourished, and she was able to meet her deadlines with ease. By decluttering her mind, Sarah unlocked her full potential and took her career to new heights.

## 2. Setting Clear and Achievable Goals

Once you've decluttered your environment and mind, the next step is to set clear and achievable goals. The process of setting goals becomes much more effective when you're operating from a place of clarity and focus.

**Practical Advice:**

- **SMART Goals:** The SMART framework is a well-known method for setting clear and achievable goals. SMART stands for Specific, Measurable, Achievable, Relevant, and Time-bound. By setting SMART goals, you can create a clear roadmap for success and track your progress along the way.

- **Break Down Big Goals:** Large goals can be overwhelming and difficult to achieve all at once. Break them down into smaller, manageable tasks that can be completed step by step. This approach not only makes the goal more achievable but also gives you a sense of accomplishment as you complete each task.

- **Visualize Your Success:** Visualization is a powerful tool for goal achievement. Take time to visualize yourself achieving your goals—what does it look like, feel like, and mean to you? This mental exercise can reinforce your commitment to your goals and motivate you to take consistent action.

**Story Example:** *Mark's Journey to Clear Goals*

Mark, a sales executive, had always set ambitious goals for his career, but he often found himself falling short. His goals were vague, such as "increase sales" or "grow the business," which left him feeling lost and unsure of how to proceed. After learning about the SMART framework, Mark decided to apply it to his goal-setting process.

He set a specific goal to "increase sales by 20% within the next six months by focusing on customer retention and upselling." This goal was specific, measurable, and time-bound, making it easier for Mark to track his progress. He broke the goal down into actionable steps, such as developing a customer retention strategy and training his team on upselling techniques.

By setting a clear and achievable goal, Mark was able to focus his efforts and work towards it with determination. The results were impressive—within six months, he not only achieved his goal but exceeded it, increasing sales by 25%. Mark's experience taught him the importance of setting clear goals and the power of decluttering his approach to success.

## 3. Creating an Action Plan—From Vision to Reality

Setting goals is only the first step; the next step is to create an action plan to turn your vision into reality. An action plan provides a clear roadmap for achieving your goals, outlining the specific steps you need to take and the timeline for completion.

**Practical Advice:**

- **Create a Step-by-Step Plan:** Break your goals down into specific, actionable steps. Each step should be clear and concise, with a timeline for completion. This plan serves as a roadmap, guiding you from where you are now to where you want to be.

- **Stay Flexible:** While it's important to have a plan, it's equally important to remain flexible. Life is unpredictable, and you may encounter obstacles along the way. Be willing to adjust your plan as needed, while keeping your ultimate goal in mind.

- **Track Your Progress:** Regularly monitor your progress towards your goals. This not only keeps you accountable but also allows you to celebrate small victories along the way. Tracking progress can also help you identify areas where you may need to make adjustments or put in extra effort.

**Story Example:** *Emily's Action Plan for Success*

Emily, a small business owner, had a clear vision for expanding her business, but she wasn't sure how to turn that vision into reality. She knew she needed to increase her online presence, develop new products, and improve customer service, but the tasks seemed overwhelming.

To tackle this challenge, Emily created a detailed action plan. She started by breaking down her goal into specific steps, such as "launch a new website within three months," "develop two new products by the end of the year," and "implement a customer feedback system within six months." Each step had a clear deadline and a list of tasks that needed to be completed.

Emily's action plan provided her with a clear roadmap to success. By focusing on one step at a time, she was able to make steady progress towards her goal. Within a year, Emily had successfully launched her new website, introduced new products, and enhanced her customer service, resulting in significant business growth. Her action plan turned her vision into reality, demonstrating the power of a structured approach to goal achievement.

## 4. The Role of Consistency and Persistence

Consistency and persistence are key to achieving your goals. Even the best plans can fail if they're not followed through with consistent action. Decluttering your life helps you maintain the focus and determination needed to stay on track, even when challenges arise.

**Practical Advice:**

- **Develop Daily Habits:** Success is often the result of small, consistent actions taken over time. Develop daily habits that align with your goals, such as setting aside time each day to work on your most important tasks or reviewing your goals each morning to stay focused.

- **Stay Motivated:** Motivation can wane over time, so it's important to find ways to stay inspired. This could include setting up a reward system for reaching milestones, finding an accountability partner, or regularly revisiting your vision to remind yourself of why you started.

- **Embrace Setbacks as Learning Opportunities:** Setbacks are a natural part of any journey to success. Instead of viewing them as failures, embrace them as opportunities to learn and grow. Analyze what went wrong, make adjustments, and keep moving forward with renewed determination.

**Story Example:** *David's Path to Persistence*

David, an aspiring novelist, had a dream of writing a best-selling book. However, the demands of his day job and family responsibilities made it difficult for him to find time to write. Despite these challenges, David was determined to achieve his goal.

He decided to develop a daily writing habit, committing to write for at least 30 minutes every morning before work. There were days when the words flowed easily, and others when it felt like a struggle, but David persisted. He also found ways to stay motivated, such as joining a writing group for accountability and setting small rewards for reaching word count milestones.

Over time, David's consistency paid off. He completed the first draft of his novel and continued to revise and improve it. Although the journey was long and filled with challenges,

David's persistence eventually led to success. His novel was published and received critical acclaim, proving that consistency and determination are essential ingredients for achieving any goal.

## 5. Celebrating Success and Reflecting on Your Journey

Achieving your goals is a significant accomplishment, and it's important to take the time to celebrate your success. Reflecting on your journey can also provide valuable insights that will help you set and achieve even bigger goals in the future.

**Practical Advice:**

- **Celebrate Your Achievements:** When you reach a goal, take the time to celebrate. Whether it's a small victory or a major milestone, acknowledging your success reinforces positive behaviour and motivates you to keep going.

- **Reflect on Your Journey:** After achieving a goal, reflect on the journey that led you there. What strategies worked well? What challenges did you overcome? Reflecting on these questions can provide valuable lessons for future goal-setting and achievement.

- **Set New Goals:** Success is a continuous journey, not a final destination. Once you've achieved a goal, set new ones that challenge you to grow and evolve. The process of setting and achieving goals is an ongoing cycle that keeps you moving forward.

**Story Example:** *Lisa's Reflection on Success*

Lisa, a marathon runner, had set a goal to qualify for the Boston Marathon—a challenging feat that required months of rigorous training. After achieving her goal and crossing the finish line in Boston, Lisa took time to reflect on her journey. She realized that the key to her success was not just physical training but also mental preparation and consistency.

Lisa celebrated her achievement with friends and family, but she didn't stop there. She set new goals for herself, including running marathons in other cities and mentoring new runners. By reflecting on her success and setting new challenges, Lisa continued to push herself to new heights, proving that the journey to success is never truly over.

www.ingramcontent.com/pod-product-compliance
Lightning Source LLC
Chambersburg PA
CBHW061335250726
48657CB00004B/1175